Symbolism in Chinese Food

SYMBOLISM IN CHINESE FOOD

Kog-Hwang I-Ling

Graham Brash
Singapore

First published in 1991 by
Graham Brash (Pte) Ltd
227 Rangoon Road
Singapore 0821

ISBN 9971-49-248-2

Photographs by the author
Cover design by K. H. Teo
Typeset by Quaser Technology Pte Ltd
Printed in Singapore by Utopia Press

Contents

1. Introduction

For centuries, the Chinese people have placed emphasis on the business of cooking and eating. Great emphasis is also given to the cultural significance and symbolism of the food they eat. Much of the knowledge about the symbolic significance of Chinese food has been handed down from one generation to another, chiefly by word of mouth. So our understanding today of the cultural symbolism of the Chinese food served during festivals and family celebrations is a combination of the things which the older members of the family can remember plus the adaptations of the modern Chinese people.

Food has cultural significance universally. We have learnt the eating of hot cross buns and Easter eggs as well as Christmas turkey and pudding from the West. At the day-to-day level, people entertain and celebrate their successes with food and they also exchange gifts of food with relatives and friends.

In most cultures therefore, food has a social function. At its most basic, food brings people together. The Chinese lunar new year family reunion dinner is relatively well-known as is the Malay *kenduri* or village-wide gathering to celebrate a wedding. Bringing people together is, however, only one of the many cultural functions of food. The offer of food often serves as a goodwill gesture and symbol of regard. In many local sociological surveys of neighbourhoods in Singapore, the exchange of gifts of food among Chinese and other ethnic groups is used as a measure of the intensity and level of relations among neighbours. For the Chinese, the exchange of gifts of food is culturally symbolic. This exchange of food shows that the givers have more than the basic necessities and wish to share good things with others. Gifts of food are frequently exchanged among the Chinese of today especially during the many festivals which are still celebrated.

The strongest reason for a book on the cultural significance of Chinese food is the awareness of the possibility that it will all be forgotten eventually. There is little documentation on this aspect of Chinese food. Much attention has been paid to the medicinal qualities of the food eaten by the Chinese and Chinese food beliefs. A lot has been written about the *yin* (cooling) and the *yang* (hot or heaty) effects of different types of Chinese food. Less has been written about the cultural symbolism of Chinese food especially those of peasant origin.

Many types of Chinese food are culturally symbolic. They make up the offerings during religious festivals and are used in entertaining or as gifts. Several kinds of Chinese food which have cultural symbolism may no longer be available today. Not only have popular tastes changed but many of the old-style cooks, confectioners and tradespeople have disappeared and the secrets and skills required for the preparation of the food have gone with them. In addition, many types of food which are culturally symbolic and still readily available today, now come in new packaging and appear very different from their original versions.

There is, therefore, more to the cultural symbolism of Chinese food than the reasons behind their origins and their importance among the Chinese people. Many types of food may not be found in recipe books because of their relative obscurity and humble origins. The information in this book has been based on knowledge of Chinese food served during festivities past and present. Interviews with housewives, hawkers, tradespeople and shopkeepers were also conducted.

In the course of gathering materials for the book, the author also discovered that there were many Chinese food-buffs who were unaware of the existence of several types of Chinese food of importance in the celebration of Chinese festivals. People from different dialect groups and originally from different provinces in mainland China celebrate festivals with quite dissimilar types of food. In the process of compiling this book, the author also developed a lively appreciation of the capacity of the Chinese food culture for change. It is a culture which is still very traditional but is also highly receptive to modern and foreign influences. This characteristic of Chinese food, which must be as old as the hills of China, is probably one of the reasons behind its continued popularity today.

The kinds of food which will be discussed in the book can be considered as literally the footnotes to great Chinese cuisine. Many are of peasant ancestry and also immigrant Chinese origins. They were not the kinds of food served at grand banquets for the nobility and gentry in the past. This does not mean that the food was not good. Like acupuncture, many things Chinese, which have received international recognition, are reportedly of peasant origins.

The kinds of food which are to be discussed have probably become popular because they can be prepared quickly and taste good even when cooked in large quantities. In the past, it was necessary to cook in large amounts in order to feed large and hungry families plus all the different generations of relatives who usually gathered together for family celebrations and festivals. Originally, much of the food must have been prepared for people who were more often than not, farmers and labourers. They were people with hearty appetites and a preference for plain but plentiful food rather than food with trimmings and frills.

People who travelled in China in the past reported contrasts in the types of meals which peasants and ordinary Chinese ate. Some described the poverty among the peasants who had to struggle to find enough to eat, with rice as the occasional treat and sweet potato as the staple. The travellers have marvelled at the splendid results which the Chinese have been able to get out of their farms in spite of the small size of the plots and the poor farm implements available. Still other travellers spoke of the meals they shared with peasants and which were made up of chicken broth, ducks' livers, green peas, bean shoots, shredded turkey breast, smoked venison and pork brawn with copious amounts of green tea and yellow millet wine. These were apparently the food ordinarily served among peasants and not specially cooked just for visitors.

The food discussed in this book do not include exotic items like sugar flavoured with osmanthus flowers or jams made from mauve roses which bloom during the fourth lunar month, water ices flavoured with dried orange peel, magnolia rind, cardamom and hibiscus, bears' paws, camel humps, silver woodears or monkey-head mushrooms. Nor does it include food such as the dish known as "the peacock spreads its tail" which requires twenty-two processes in its preparation and fifteen ingredients including duck, ham, pork tongue, quails' eggs, crab meat and cucumber.

The food served among the ordinary Chinese have simple and relatively unassuming names. Their purpose appears to be to inform people of the ingredients or ways of cooking the food rather than titillate the palate or excite the imagination. Ordinary peasant food is not without colour or interest. Most are gaily decorated with ingredients such as Chinese parsley or coriander leaves, fried shallots, spring onions, red chillies or egg strips. These garnishings are both decorative as well as good to eat, adding to the flavour of the food. Tables laden with food offerings during Chinese festivals are usually very colourful and add to the gaiety of the celebrations.

What must be especially memorable about the food served during celebrations in the past was the number of people who were involved in the preparation of the food. Chinese people have long believed not only in growing and harvesting the food together, but also cooking and eating together, from the same dish. Feasts were prepared with the help of all family members, young and old, big and small, male and female. All this participation put everyone in a festive mood. While some helped cook the food, others would be running out to get that last minute ingredient. Many shopkeepers stayed above their shops then and could be persuaded to stay open till the very last second before they launched their own celebrations. Things have, of course, changed now. Chinese families are largely nuclear and small in comparison to the families in the past. When there are large family gatherings, these are more likely to be held in restaurants.

The ingredients used in the food served during family celebrations and festivals among the ordinary people are significant not only because of their abundance and versatility but also their commonness and humble origins. Emphasis is apparently not on the ingredients alone but the effort put into fashioning the food into dishes fit for the gods worshipped by the Chinese.

The common Chinese people had limited food resources to feed their large families in the past but these constraints have been turned into an advantage. This is apparent in the wide range of dishes which have been prepared from the simplest of ingredients through a variety of cooking methods. The food used in celebrations thus also reminds us of the creativity of the past generations of Chinese. As immigrants they have had to adapt to new resources while still striving to preserve food traditions. They were adept at incorporating local ingredients into their food. The evidence is seen in the variety of *peranakan* dishes which have been included in Chinese celebrations today. For most Chinese, learning to cook new dishes and adapting food of other ethnic groups into their diets meant more than a lifestyle trend, food fad or cultivating a cosmopolitan outlook on food. It has meant keeping food traditions alive and ever increasing in variety and interest.

Chinese chefs and cooks in general were also ingenious in their use of cooking utensils. Clay, wooden, ceramic and enamelled meal containers were used in the preparation and serving of food. Whatever was available appeared to have been used and rice bowls for instance were used for many types of cakes. Specifically, there are the rice bowl cakes, so-called because they are steamed in small rice bowls.

In this book, the types of food which are still popular and those which are no longer so commonly seen during Chinese celebrations and festivals are featured. Food that are part of the daily meals of Chinese are also included mainly because they can be prepared from ingredients similar to those used in ceremonial offerings. The selection is not exhaustive. Documenting all the different types of Chinese food and their cultural symbolism would be a task beyond the scope of this book. Instead, the book concentrates on Hokkien dishes and food. The author's familiarity with Cantonese, Teochew, Hakka and Shanghainese food has convinced her that they have a lot in common with Hokkien food. Granted there are differences because of the availability of ingredients since each dialect group originated from a different province in mainland China. The ingenuity at improvisation among the Chinese is seen in the wide diversity of dishes and cooking methods which is their legacy.

The Food Legacy of the Chinese

Chinese dishes have been divided into local, minor, national, court, government and monastery dishes. Local dishes have been classified sometimes into eight and at other times, three, four or five major styles of food preparation. Such differentiation is based on provincial variations in climate, food products and the customs of each place. The eight major styles of cooking have been identified as Shandung, Sichuan, Jiangsu, Guangdung,

Zhejiang, Fujian, Hunan and Anhui. They are styles corresponding with broad geographical zones or regions into which mainland China can be divided. Each of the zone or region has a common climate, physical terrain and food culture. Another classification lists four main regional styles of cooking — Shandung of the region of the Huanghe (Yellow) River; Sichuan also from the Huanghe region; Jiangsu of the middle and lower reaches of the Shangjiang (Yangtze) River; and the Guangdung style of Pearl River and the southern coastal region. In this classification, the cooking from Anhui, Zhejiang, Hunan and Fujian provinces are also recognised as important provincial styles of Chinese cooking.

There is yet another classification which identifies five main regions of Chinese cooking because the Chinese reportedly favour lists of five. Hence there are five Confucian virtues, five grains, five strongly odoured foods and five savoury substances. Among the five styles is that originating from the west of China including Hunan, Sichuan and Yunnan which is the realm of hot and spicy food. There are also the coastal provinces centring on Guangzhou in the far south, which is often regarded as the greatest of Chinese regional cuisines.

Shandung dishes include food like the sweet and sour Huanghe river carp and delicious clear soups which are often parts of banquets. There are also the Beijing mutton fondue which used to be cooked with 1500 fire pots and the famous Beijing roast duck. This was originally roasted over the burning wood of peach, jujube or date trees, which gave off a special fragrance with relatively little smoke. Shandung food is delicate and famous for its fragrance and pure tastes. With the difficulties of cultivating food, the Shandung farmers rely on the sweet potato as a staple. In tough times they were deemed fortunate to be able to eat sweet potatoes three meals a day, one potato per meal. The sweet potato remains important today not only in Shandung cooking but in Chinese food culture.

Sichuan dishes are rich and spicy as the region has large stretches of fertile agricultural land. Although not native to China, spices like the chilli, have been incorporated into China food. The spices have come to distinguish Chinese cooking as if they were China's own. The Sichuan style of cooking is among the oldest, having apparently originated in the Qin dynasty of 221-201 B.C. Famous Sichuan dishes include the peppery hot beancurd, the *ma bo fu*. This dish was reputedly named after a pock-marked woman who was extremely good at preparing the dish.

Guangdung dishes provide the flavours of south China and to quote a Chinese poet, one should be "born in Suzhou, live in Hangzhou, die in Luzhou and eat in Guangzhou." This is because the most beautiful women in China are said to be found in Suzhou while Hangzhou has the country's finest silk and the wood in Luzhou is said to be the best for making coffins. Guangzhou, of course, is where the best cooks and food are to be found in China. The Cantonese adore fresh seafood, preferably still swimming and they have contributed among other things, *dim sum* to Chinese cuisine. *Dim sum* literally means "to touch the heart" and comprise countless varieties of light snacks which are eaten with Chinese tea. The meal is usually referred to as *yum cha* which means "drinking tea". *Dim sum* cooking enables the Chinese to cook a meal of several dishes and yet use the fuel, time and effort for one.

The invitation to *yum cha* is symbolic among the Chinese as it extends hospitality and is a gesture of goodwill. Guests are invited to drink or "eat" tea. The term "eat tea" also refers to the tea ceremony of Chinese weddings when the newlyweds offer cups of tea to and are formally acknowledged by the elders in the family. The importance of tea in Chinese culture is also seen in its use during important festivals like the Chinese lunar new year celebrations. Flowers such as the chrysanthemum which symbolises the full year, are used to make tea which is served during the new year celebrations. Extreme economy was practised in the use of tea leaves. Used tea leaves would be boiled for mouth-wash after which they would be dried and used to stuff pillows as they were found to be extremely cooling in the summer.

Zhejiang dishes include the famous Yangzhou fried rice and the meatball known as Lion's Head. There is the famous Shaoxing wine and from Shanghai comes the much sought-after hairy crabs. The emphasis appears to be on the skills in cutting up the ingredients. This emphasis is shared by most types of Chinese cooking. Food is cut into small pieces or sliced thinly. Slicing has been perfected into a fine art not only to achieve subtlety of flavour but also to stretch the ingredients as far as possible.

While not often mentioned among the major regional styles of cooking, there are well-known Hakka dishes like the salt-baked chicken. As the Hakka people travelled so much and settled in many different provinces in the south of China, they often carried their food with them and salt was used extensively in their cooking.

Apart from local styles of cooking described above, there are dishes created by ethnic minorities, imperial cooks and those working for civil and military officials of high rank and pay in the past. Finally, there are monastery dishes comprising vegetarian food, reportedly numbering some 100 types.

The food legacy also includes different methods of cooking. Twenty-two methods have been listed — stir-frying, stir-frying in a little oil over a low flame, deep-frying, deep-frying to a brown colour and quick frying in hot oil and spiced sauce, mixing spiced seasoning into boiled ingredients, split-second deep-frying with highly seasoned sauce over a high flame, coating deep-fried ingredients with a slippery sauce, frying ingredients coated with an egg and cornflour mixture in a little oil over a low flame, baking in a little oil, braising, braising pre-cooked ingredients in a thick sauce, garnishing braised ingredients with a sauce, steaming, steaming or simmering in a covered pot, simmering, boiling, cooking quickly in boiling water, roasting or baking, mixing with seasoning for a cold dish, smoking, stewing in soya sauce and stewing with soya sauce and spices. In addition, there are three other methods of preparing sweet dishes — dipping in melted sugar, preserving in syrup and coating with melted sugar. Though diverse, the styles and methods of cooking have been handed down through generations and are not only testimony to the ingenuity and resourcefulness of Chinese cooks but also the legacy of all Chinese.

The Significance of Food and Eating in Chinese Speech

The frequent reference to food and food containers in conversations among Chinese of all dialect groups is further proof of the cultural significance and symbolism of food among the Chinese people. Although the references are less in use today, they remain a significant illustration of the cultural importance of food among the Chinese.

A common greeting among the Chinese is "Have you eaten?" or "Have you eaten rice yet?" Employment is referred to as a person's rice bowl and earning a living as "working for three meals a day". Meaningless conversation is compared to empty food baskets while confusion is expressed as ignorance of the kind of bowl cakes being talked about.

The person doing the marketing in the house and handling the household budget is known as the one carrying the vegetable basket. This can be any household member although the position of carrying the vegetable basket is considered an important one, with enhanced status. Both men and women can carry the vegetable or shopping basket.

In telling off the young who think they know more, the older family members often say that they have eaten more salt than the young have eaten rice. This means that the older people have far more experience about life than the younger people. Many young girls have pledged to eat rice *congee* and salt with the poor men they love as an avowal of their determination to face hardship and difficulty.

Other similes like those concerning the wasteful eating of rice refer to the undertaking of futile tasks. Greedy children are also compared with wives who start to scold their husbands immediately when their mouths are empty and there is nothing more to eat. Guests talk about breaking the rice pots or bowls of their hosts. The breaking of bowls and cups on auspicious days are still considered a bad omen. Children are also taught not to stick their chopsticks in their rice bowls or clatter the chopsticks against their bowls as these actions resemble those of beggars. Another custom calls for the adding of bowls and chopsticks to the household utensils every Chinese lunar new year to symbolise increase and prosperity. Fujian Chinese consider it the good life to be able to eat *poh loon* (菠菜), an expensive vegetable, and dress in silk all the time.

The taste and other qualities of food are also used in similes which describe people's characters. Suave and smooth-talking people are referred to as oily or sweet mouth. A lack of food ingredients (没有料) refers to people without stamina or ability. Weakness is compared to *doufu*. Eating vinegar suggests envy and a jealous person. People who are in the way are referred to as "eating onion". Those who have joined the nunnery or monastery are those who are "eating vegetables", doubtless referring to their vegetarian diets.

There is a Chinese equivalent for the bad apple. This is the bad egg or smelly duck's egg. Where the West has its peaches and cream complexions, the Chinese favour skins as white and as soft as flour. The Chinese have their equivalent of being "fed up". They would say that they feel full just looking at or listening to something they dislike. The Chinese "as easy as eating peanuts" needs no explanation.

The names of food and food containers are also used in terms of endearment as well. So the farmer in Pearl S. Buck's novel *Good Earth*, called his wife "my turnip". "My stove" or "pot" is commonly used among the Fujian people to refer to their children. "Silly melon" or "silly winter melon" is used to fondly chide children who are behaving foolishly. There are innumerable other examples of puns which provide many kinds of food with their cultural symbolism. As the names of these types of food sound like words with auspicious meaning, the food has become important during Chinese festivals and family celebrations. These are illustrated in the following sections.

Chinese Food and Festivities

Similar to festivities in other cultures, Chinese festivals are celebrations with lots of food and drink. Much of the fun and merrymaking revolve around eating and drinking. Shakespeare's Falstaff and Bacchus of Greek mythology, would have been very much at home at a Chinese festival or family celebration. Many Chinese celebrations are not religious, being rather more the demonstration of their appreciation for good food and eating.

Past generations of Chinese had many festivals to observe and even more deities and ancestors to venerate. Not only were there major festivals but also monthly offerings of food to the "deities at the back of the house" which the Chinese people believed to be homeless spirits roaming the realm without any family or friends to venerate them with regular offerings of food. The imagination and creativity of the cooks in large families of the past must have been severely tested. Today's Chinese people are the fortunate beneficiaries of the triumphs of these cooks. Most of the food traditionally served during celebrations remain popular and have withstood the test of time and the coming and going of food fads. The popularity of the food today has remained although the superstitions and rituals which brought them into existence in the first place have long been forgotten. Nevertheless, the food and their cultural significance are in themselves symbols of the tenacity of a people from a past filled with hunger, famines and the constant threat of starvation.

The observation has been made that those who cannot believe what the Chinese eat will be less incredulous if they had as many mouths to eat. They too, would suddenly find that all sorts of food which had previously been considered inedible, could be eaten as well. Through food, it has been shown how the Chinese have developed the art of necessity which remains an integral part of the Chinese way of doing things. If given the choice between a perfect pear and a mangy one, so one author has written, no Chinese would hesitate to reach for perfection. That choice, however, seldom existed and thus, a lively imagination was brought to bear on the imperfections of the world.

Outsiders have marvelled at the numerous family feasts, banquets, festivals of the summer and winter equinoxes, weddings and anniversaries, birthdays of gods and goddesses not only of Chinese religions but also imported faiths like Buddhism, Islam and Christianity, successful business deals and the launching of businesses and agreements which have been the occasions for celebration with food and drink. Food which are culturally symbolic are served not only during such major celebrations but also during the visits of friends. There are also no age barriers at these celebrations. Both old and young participate.

The three greatest festivals for the Chinese are purportedly the first day of the first lunar month which is the Chinese lunar new year or Lantern Festival. Then comes the fifth day of the fifth lunar month which is the Dragon Boat Festival. Finally, on the fifteenth day of the eighth lunar month, there is the Mid-Autumn or Moon Festival. Whatever the occasion being celebrated, a lot of effort still goes into ascertaining that all the food that are symbolic, are being prepared. Shopping for the ingredients usually starts a few weeks before a major celebration. In the past, there would be times when nobody would know the occasion or festival being celebrated unless the food being served was right for the occasion. Indeed, the food distinguished wedding celebrations from say, birthdays and even funerals.

There are still differences in opinion and practice among the dialect groups about the symbolism of various kinds of food offerings. Such differences can be sources of conflict. Hokkien parents, for example, would have been shocked at the suggestion of presenting roast pigs as presents to Teochew families of their future daughters-in-law. The Hokkien people only present roast pigs to their parents-in-law as funeral gifts.

Younger members of the family were expected to remember the dates of important events such as the birthdays of the older members of the family. The womenfolk were also expected to remember the dates of major festivals as they were the ones who did the preparation and cooking.

The quality and the quantity of the food which the Chinese served or failed to served their friends during celebrations demonstrated their regard for these friends publicly, regardless of what they may think of these friends in private. Friends who visited were seldom allowed to leave without ample refreshments. In the past, the children in the house have been known to be told to leave the better food for guests.

Chinese celebrations are also occasions for ostentatious display of wealth. Much of this display would be in the form of the types of food served to friends and relatives or presented as gifts. The kinds of dishes served, the restaurants used and the number of dishes and tables provided remain measures of the substance of the hosts during Chinese celebrations.

This book also illustrates the ideals, hopes and aspirations of Chinese people which are contained in the symbolism attached to their food. Prosperity, achievements, having lots of children, family unity, happiness and longevity are just some of the hopes and aspirations which are part of the symbolic value of Chinese food offerings. These food offerings symbolise the things which have been important to generations of Chinese. In many instances they are things which remain important to the Chinese of today.

PART ONE

FOOD FOR FESTIVALS AND SOCIAL OCCASIONS

2.   Engagement Or Wedding Biscuits And Desserts

It seems auspicious to begin with wedding celebrations and the "four-coloured" (四色饼) Chinese biscuits which are used as gifts during Chinese wedding engagements. Traditional Chinese celebrations are extremely elaborate. Preparations start months before the chosen date. A number of rounds of gifts of food and other items from the bridegroom to the bride is involved. These form part of the bride price while the distribution of gifts of food to friends also serves to announce the pending nuptials. The Reverend Justus Doolittle in his 1864 book on the *Social Life of the Chinese* described an elaborate presentation of wedding cakes even among the poor and the lower classes of Chinese society in Foochow at that time. According to Reverend Justus, the number of these "cakes of ceremony" varied from several score to several hundreds. The cakes used were round, about an inch thick, weighing about one pound and ten or twelve ounces each and measured nearly a foot in diameter. These cakes were made of wheat flour with a filling made from sugar, lard and small pieces of fat pork. They are apparently a sort of mince pie. These are the large cakes of ceremony. In addition, other kinds of food were presented including five kinds of dried fruits, several kinds of small cakes, a cock and a hen, a gander and a goose. The top one of the various stacks of these wedding cakes was usually decorated with several small dolls fashioned out of wheat flour and fastened on slips of bamboo. Each of these dolls was a few inches high. The wedding cakes were usually distributed among relatives and intimate friends of the bride's family.

A few days before the wedding, the family of the bridegroom would send food again to the family of the bride. For this occasion, the food items included a cock and a hen, a leg of a pig and a goat, eight small cakes of bread and a quantity of vermicelli. Part of the food including the cock had to be eaten by the bride on the morning of her marriage. On each of the bread cakes would be a large red character made from dough, in an ancient form of writing with an auspicious meaning such as, longevity, happiness, official emoluments or joy. Four of these cakes might have four characters on them instead of one. These would be phrases meaning "the phoenixes are singing in concert" or "the ducks are seeking their mates". The bread cakes and vermicelli signify good omens. The former described by Reverend Justus Doolittle seem to resemble the *mee koo*, steamed bread which is a common festive food offering today. Chinese characters with auspicious meanings are still moulded on these breads when they are used as festival offerings. Although the cake presentation ceremonies are no longer so elaborate, many of the types of food used in the past are still a part of Chinese wedding rituals.

Until the end of the last dynasty, the six rites laid down for a marriage were followed strictly by the Chinese (Lee Siow Mong in *The Spectrum of Chinese Culture*). Today, the rites are still followed in modified forms. The first rite was the acceptance of a present by the girl's family to show they were prepared to consider the proposal. This was *na cai* (纳采) and the present was usually a goose. The second rite was *wen ming* (问名), or literally, "asking the name". At this time, the girl's particulars and name are given by the go-between to the boy's family. After the horoscopes of the couple have been considered, there is the third rite, the *na ji* (纳吉) meaning the "acceptance of the propitious" which is the betrothal. The fourth rite is *na cheng* (纳征) or "acceptance of evidence" which involves the exchange of gifts of food and other things. The fifth rite is *qing qi* (请期) or "asking the date" while the final rite is *ying qing* (迎亲), that of "receiving the bride".

Even today, the Chinese biscuits used as gifts that are part of wedding celebrations are not quite the regular Arnott's or Khong Guan (both large-scale biscuit manufacturing firms) biscuits which are popular today and it is most unlikely that they are sold in supermarkets. It is more likely for one to find these biscuits in the old-style Chinese bakeries and biscuit shops. Despite their name, these *ko-piah* (糕饼) or *ko-ah lau huay* as the biscuits are often also referred to, are not of four different colours. Rather, they are four different kinds of biscuits which the bridegroom is expected to send over to the bride's family together with other gifts like the wine, leg of pork and dowry on an auspicious day suitably distant from the actual wedding day. The exact date is specially chosen after consultations with the geomancer. Although this custom was a must in the past, it is more flexible nowadays and many prefer to do without it. Others have changed the kinds of food offered and opted for cream cakes instead of the traditional biscuits.

For the Chinese who have preserved the custom, the range of different types of biscuits prescribed is wide. So the types of biscuits which are used can vary, depending on the bridegroom's budget and the demands of his bride's family. The only condition is that the biscuits should be sweet and their colouring auspicious since the occasion is a happy one. These biscuits are then distributed together with the wedding invitations to relatives and guests.

One of the different kinds of biscuits which are often used is the peanut brittle (豆仁方). These are slabs of caramel used to coat crunchy, roasted peanuts that are tightly packed together. The rectangular-shaped biscuits are usually also covered with sesame seeds on one side.

Also popular are the sweet bean biscuits (豆糕). The shapes of these types of biscuits vary and they can be square, round or six-sided. These biscuits are usually pink and white and Chinese characters denoting "good luck" are often used to decorate them.

Other biscuits which are commonly presented are the roundish biscuits of flaky pastry with a sweet filling which is made from mung beans (豆沙饼). The marks of the seals of the biscuit-makers are often stamped in red on the biscuits. These mung bean biscuits are presented in many different ways. They are either sold singly or packed in fives in grease-proof paper. There is a miniature version of these biscuits which originated in Penang and are known there locally as *Tambun* biscuits. Unlike the larger variety, these miniature mung bean biscuits are not commonly presented as gifts before a wedding. Each dialect group actually has its own version of mung bean biscuits and there are as many varieties as there are dialect groups.

Equally popular as wedding gifts from the bridegroom to the bride are the *muay lau* and *lau huay* (麻茗,米茗), cylindrically-shaped biscuits made from glutinous rice and which are either covered in roasted sesame seeds or gaily coloured rice crispies. These biscuits are still popular and can usually be found in old-style Chinese bakeries. They are fragrant and are splendid with Chinese tea. Another type of wedding biscuit which is also popular is the *bee pang* or rice planks. These are sugar coated rice crispies resembling the *lau huay*. Like the *lau huay*, the rice grains used to make the *bee pang* are also coloured red and white.

Another type of biscuit which is also used for wedding gifts is the *pong pia* (膨饼) which literally means the "puffed-up biscuit". This biscuit is made of soft biscuit dough and the top has a sprinkling of roasted sesame seeds. The biscuit is not popular among people with dentures because of its stickiness.

There are more delicate kinds of sweet, wafer-like biscuits fashioned to look like money pouches and although not made of the same ingredients as love-letters (旦揩饼), which are also known as egg rolls, there is a resemblance. Nowadays, commercially made versions of this biscuit are available in several colours besides the usual beige and they are usually left in their original round shapes rather than folded like they were used to. The egg rolls are still popular during Chinese lunar new year celebrations. While some are rolled into little cylinders, others are folded. These biscuits have been part of Chinese lunar new year celebrations for a long time.

Confectioners in the traditional types of bakeries can still remember the ceremony which is called *phua tow* during which gifts of biscuits and preserves such as red dates and candied winter melon sticks are presented to the bride's family on an auspicious day before the wedding to celebrate the coming of age and gaining of adulthood by the wedding couple. It is possible that this ceremony is no longer observed and it may have been simplified in modern times with a version known as the *chuin tow* during which no food is involved. There are dialect variations, however. The Cantonese observe the ceremony by having the wedding couple comb their hair. Hokkiens celebrate it with the guests witnessing a walk round the bed by the wedding couple in ceremonial dress. This is done after the couple has offered prayers to the ancestors, while kneeling on a large woven bamboo tray that is used for winnowing.

While these gifts of wedding biscuits continue to be an important part of the celebrations, the Chinese of today are just as likely to present Western-style cakes and confectioneries to their wedding guests. There used to be more than a hundred types of these biscuits. Their number has dwindled. The biscuits are, however, still being made and sold in Chinese biscuit shops, unlike a wedding dessert which is now no longer served.

Although a savoury version of *bee tie bak* (米潲目) is still eaten today, its sweet version is no longer popular. It was a Chinese wedding dessert that was all the rage in the 1950s and 1960s. This dessert has been replaced in popularity by dishes such as canned longans (a type of Chinese fruit) and maraschino cherries. It has therefore become another victim of the vagaries of fashion and is seldom seen and hardly remembered. Looking very much like *chendol* (the authentic kind which is flavoured with a local grass herb called *pandan* leaf and not the mass-produced and flavourless version dyed to resemble the original, with green food colouring, that goes by the same name today), the *bee tie bak* are actually slim, needle-shaped pieces of rice flour. For the wedding dessert, it is usually coloured pink and white and sometimes yellow, making it a colourful ending to the wedding feast. They are then cooked in sugar syrup and served chilled which makes it a refreshing dessert. What actually is eaten as a savoury form of *bee tie bak* today is definitely not the genuine item because it is a noodle going by the unfortunate and far from appetising name of "mouse droppings noodle" (老鼠粉). Although it is no longer popular as a wedding dessert, *bee tie bak* is still being sold by hawkers plying in the smaller towns of Malaysia.

As mentioned above, a wedding desert, which is more commonly encountered today, is tinned longans in sugar syrup. There is a Hokkien saying which essentially claims that those who eat longans must have a good ending. The proverb (俗语) rhymes and goes like " 吃龙眼好晚景 ". During most Chinese festivals and celebrations, sweet desserts are usually served at the end of the meal to symbolise sweet and happy endings. A variety of cold and hot desserts are still served, some of which are more commonly featured than the others.

Biscuits, Confectionery and Savouries for Friends and Festivals

Biscuits and cakes are important in Chinese diets. Cakes are common festival offerings. The shapes and colours of these cakes and biscuits were as significant as their taste. Generally, they are round or eight-sided. Biscuits or cakes served or presented as gifts during the Chinese lunar new year are usually round like the almond shortbread for example or biscuits made of lard and white sugar. During the Chinese lunar new year celebrations of the past, mothers of families usually offered their children small cakes with the wish that they will *pu-pu kao-sheng* (步步高升), meaning "rise gradually to eminence (finally becoming a high official)". There is a pun on the word *kao* (糕) which sounds like the word meaning lofty (高) and setting a high aim for oneself.

The bounties of frying and baking

There have been varieties of biscuits and cakes that were either Chinese in origin or popular among the Chinese but many are seldom seen or eaten these days. While some retain their symbolic significance, they are still popular mainly because they are relatively inexpensive treats for the occasion when the family is eating out or having a late night supper or when many friends are visiting the home. Although the *yu-tiao* (油条) or Chinese cruellers are ubiquitous in hawker centres and have even made it to the big time in hotel restaurants of large cities, it is more difficult to find the other varieties of fried flour dumplings, like the *kup choong*, glutinous rice patties wrapped in the same dough used for another version of this flour dumpling known as the *hum chim pang* (咸煎饼). These flour dumplings are deep-fried pastries which are still immensely popular as a breakfast food among the Chinese.

The *yu-tiao*, so the legend goes, originated after a sad episode in China's history during which a villain successfully plotted and brought about the downfall and death of a Chinese national hero, Yue Fei, who was much revered for his love of the country, filial piety and integrity. Making a pastry which the Hokkien called by a name sounding like that of the villain, Ching Kuei, and then deep-frying it provided the peasant Chinese with the means of going through the motion of punishing the villain everyday in the way they would have liked to have done but would not have had the opportunity of doing otherwise. In Hokkien the *yu-tiao* is called *yu char kuei* which literally means "fried kuei". As the story went, after Ching Kuei's treachery became known, groups of highly amused people were gathered around the street hawkers, who had cleverly fashioned small pieces of dough each into the shape of a man resembling Ching Kuei and were frying them. When questioned by Ching Kuei's soldiers, the street hawkers covered up by inviting the soldiers to try their new pastry. Doubtless, the crowds of Yue Fei sympathisers and street hawkers derived some satisfaction from watching the soldiers eat the fried symbol of their paymaster.

Although not many people are aware of the symbolic significance of eating *yu-tiao* today, it is still extremely popular among the Chinese today. The *yu-tiao* is a savoury pastry made from long narrow strips of flour dough which are then deep-fried. When deep-fried, the dough rises and becomes crispy just about the time it is cooked. The *yu-tiao*, sold in pairs, is an extremely versatile pastry and often serves as a dumpling as well in several dishes. It is popular with rice *congee* as it gives an extra bite to the dish; it is also an ingredient in a local sweet mung bean dessert called *tow suan*. This is cooked with mung beans in a sugar syrup which is then thickened with cornflour. *Yu-tiao* can also be stuffed with prawns and meat and then deep-fried. It is also added to a variety of clear soups.

Several Malaysians are said to hold the view that there is no taste in the world like that of *yu-tiao* dipped in Malaysian coffee, a combination which is a common breakfast meal in that part of the world. The *yu-tiao* is also an ingredient of Chinese-style *rojak* which is a salad made from different kinds of vegetables and bean curd with a sweet and chilli-flavoured sauce that is a mix of peanut sugar, ground peanuts, a local prawn paste and fermented fish paste for its dressing.

The other types of deep-fried dumplings are the *kup choong* which are also savoury. These glutinous rice and flour dumplings are less often seen than the different varieties of *hum chin pang*. These dumplings are round pastries which are made either plain, salty or with a red or black bean paste filling. The more elaborate versions are decorated with sesame seeds. There are so many varieties of deep-fried dumplings because they are also made differently by the various dialect groups. Another type is shaped like the hoof of a horse and is made from a sweet dough similar to that used for *hum chin pang*. It is made in pairs and it appears like a shorter and stumpier version of the *yu-tiao*. The name of this dumpling is none other than "horse's hoof". It remains popular for breakfast and as a snack among young and old Chinese because it is relatively inexpensive, widely available and of course, delicious, especially when it is just out of the wok and piping hot.

As it has already been pointed out earlier, the practicality of the Chinese people is evident in the names they give their food. There are biscuits which are so named because of their aftertaste rather than the ingredients they are made of. Actually, the ingredients are usually closely-guarded trade secrets. An example of these biscuits are the *chui kow saw* (脆口酥), a favourite because of its melt-in-the-mouth texture which goes very well with Chinese tea. Its name suggests that they melt in the mouth.

Other biscuits are named after their appearance. One example is the conically shaped biscuits, appropriately if not as refinedly, called the *neng-neng piah* (奶奶饼) or "breast biscuits". There are also the pig's ear biscuits (耳朵饼) which are made of rings of white biscuit which is sweet alternating with chocolate-coloured ones that are actually savoury. These appear to be a more cheaply produced treat and biscuit which looks like the savoury known as deep-fried crisps with taro cake.

Mung beans ground into a flour, form the main ingredient of the *tau ko*, which is a popular biscuit made for the celebration of the Chinese lunar new year. The biscuits are made with wooden moulds, like those bigger ones which are used to make the *ang koo kueh*. The *tau ko* biscuits are shaped into birds, fishes, flowers, turtles, shells, fans and the deities of Luck, Happiness and Prosperity.

As the Chinese people were also fond of sweet things, they have also been creative with sugar and there were several childhood treats which might have disappeared but have not been forgotten. Long gone are the childhood longings for the yards of caramel wound round a stick. Though they were disastrous for the teeth they were very good for "ever-so-long" lasting licks. Sadly, this childhood treat seems to have gone the way of the itinerant hawker, barber and the pot-mender. In the past, children and spouses who were the clinging type were often likened to caramel which was not only sweet but extremely sticky. There is a biscuit which is also not easily found or widely available these days, known as tea biscuits. They are crispy cookies actually flavoured with tea leaves. Each biscuit would be wrapped individually in white paper on which would be printed Chinese characters in green and red lettering and sold in packets.

Caramel is a versatile food and is still used as the filling of *hiong-pia* (香饼), a biscuit with a light flaky and crispy outside and the gooey caramel inside when they are freshly baked and just out of the oven, the like of which you can still find in the kitchens of small biscuit factories in Malaysia and the old-style Chinese bakeries in Singapore. The finishing touch is the sprinkling of sesame seeds on top of the biscuits. This adds to the fragrance which has given the biscuit its name, fragrant biscuit.

In the good old days, there were other healthier, five-cent childhood treats like lotus seeds (莲仔), all fresh and succulent which you popped out of the fruit holding them. Joy was getting a fruit with lots of seeds. Lotus seeds are also highly versatile and are used in several Chinese dishes, both sweet and savoury. These dishes will be discussed later. The lotus has always been associated with Buddhism and Kuan Yin, the Goddess of

Mercy. Sometimes, offerings of the lotus flower and fruit are made at the temples dedicated to the Goddess of Mercy, a vegetarian deity. These offerings are still being made especially in the homes where there are altars put up for this deity. Once, the lotus fruit could be bought, tied up in bunches of three, by elderly women farmers, who came around with their baskets hanging from sticks resting on their shoulders. The lotus seeds taste best when the fruit is tender and young. These young fruits usually have seeds that are white with light yellow centres. The bigger and older seeds would have started to germinate and they would have green shoots down their middles, making them taste bitter.

A childhood breakfast favourite of mine which is still popular now, is a featherlight pancake with a bubbly middle, over which the edges of the round pancake are folded. The whole confectionery is a melt-in-the-mouth experience which is all the more satisfying because the edges are crispy. This confectionery is not Chinese but rather an adaptation of the Indian *apong*. It resembles the Chinese pancake which is a heavier confectionery, being made of a spongy dough between which a layer of crushed groundnuts is sprinkled. Lighter versions are made of biscuit dough with a groundnut filling. The hawker will add fresh coconut in the pancake on request for that extra fragrance.

A favourite *peranakan* cake which has been much adapted by today's confectioners because its original version is seldom seen in shops, is the square of glutinous rice, *kueh salak*, white and blue, which are eaten with *kaya* or egg jam, a local variation of lemon curd since both are egg-based but flavoured differently. The egg jam is flavoured with coconut milk and pandan leaves. In addition to the home-made variety which is usually a rich golden brown in colour, there are now many commercial versions of the jam, all of which generally look pale in comparison to the home-made jam. The version which usually accompanies the kueh salak is stodgier and hence milder in flavour since flour is used to thicken the jam rather than eggs. Part of the rice used to prepare the *kueh salak* is dyed blue. Most *peranakan* cakes are not only rich but also very colourful. The *kueh salak* is made from glutinous rice which has been mixed with coconut milk and then steamed. Like other varieties of *peranakan* cakes which are made entirely of glutinous rice, the *kueh salak* is not as easily found as the other types of cakes which are prepared from rice flour. These types of cakes are discussed in the following section.

The bounties of steaming

A lot of Chinese cakes featured during Chinese festivals are steamed for a good reason, as will be seen later. An extra-large wok is usually used to accommodate the very large round bamboo steamers which can then be piled high, tier upon tier, as many as can be taken by the extra-tall wok cover used. These bamboo steamers are made to fit into the wok so that several types of cakes or dishes can be steamed at the same time, thus conserving fuel. There was often a scarcity of fuel in the past with many other demands including heating. The bamboo steamers can be piled in tiers. Usually, the dishes which require the least cooking are placed in bamboo steamers in the higher tiers while those requiring more cooking are placed in the lower tiers. One of the most popular steamed cakes is the nine-layered cake (九层糕) which requires as intricate a construction approach as the *kueh lapis* which is also a many-layered cake and just as wonderful to eat. These days one would be lucky to get more than five layers in commercial versions compared to the mandatory nine turned out by the female cooks of the past for their parents-in-law and families. The multi-layered *kueh lapis* is also popular among the Chinese because it signifies adding on or increase. Nine is a lucky number for the Chinese, signifying abundance and longevity. In the not so distant past, the rice flour mix for these nine-layered cakes used to be churned out on huge granite stone rice mills so that the more children and household members there were to help out, the faster the task was done. Where we lived the whole neighbourhood shared the stone mill which we had and which was probably the only one available for miles around. It added much festivity to the preparations for the celebration being held and gave the housewives all the reason they needed to congregate and gossip if not complain about their spouses, relatives, in-laws and ill-natured neighbours.

The rice liquid used for the steamed nine-layered cake is mixed with the just correct amount of sugar, coconut milk and food colouring in various glorious shades of pink alternating with white and then poured layer upon layer in huge aluminium trays or bamboo steamers lined with muslin that are steamed in the large woks used just for festive occasions. Use of colouring distinguishes the different layers, if the parents-in-law are

counting. This appears to be a "nonya" or *peranakan* dish
because of the addition of coconut milk. The use of
coconut milk as an ingredient makes all the dishes adapted
Chinese.

Another steamed confectionery is what can literally be
translated as an egg cake (鸡蛋糕). This is an egg and
flour sponge which experienced Chinese cooks claim
can be as light and fluffy as the amount of effort put into
beating the eggs. Before the advent of cheap electronic
goods on the market and most Chinese families were
unable to afford an electric beater, the egg mix would be
prepared in a plastic pail placed on top of an overturned
stool for hours of beating with the egg beater, which was
essentially a wire spiral coil attached to the end of a long
wooden handle. Like the preparation of the ground rice
mixture used in other cakes, this is the kind of work
which calls for the contribution of the children in the
family. The egg mixture is then poured into a bamboo
steamer lined with muslin, the size of the basket varying
with the size of the egg cake being prepared. When the
sponge has been steamed, the fissures appearing on the
top of the cake are symbolic of prosperity and luck
(福). Some housewives refuse to make the cake in case
there are no fissures after steaming and bad luck de-
scends on the house. The cake is a regular food offering
during Chinese festivals and although a nice warm beige
colour when it is cooked because of the steamed egg
mixture, it is also dotted with little dabs of red food
colouring for luck. Artistry for the children was putting
on these dabs of colouring with the round ends of a
chopstick dipped in food dye.

There are several steamed savoury egg dishes which are popular among the Chinese. Despite the scare about high cholesterol levels and salmonella, eggs remain important in Chinese diets. Apart from their symbolic value, eggs are also believed to be capable of putting roses into children's cheeks and many elderly women still recommend eggs for pregnant women. Eggs are whisked up with water and then poured into minced pork in which are bits of salted egg and preserved radish, before steaming. The same egg mix can be poured into chopped up root vegetables and then steamed. Preserved radish is also good chopped up and then mixed into an omelette. Omelettes are also cooked in a sweet and sour sauce to which sliced red chillies and big onions are added. Eggs are also added to soups to thicken them and add to the flavour and as will be seen later hard-boiled eggs are important in many Chinese festival dishes. For Shanghainese farmers, eggs are food which give them strong heads the way they find bamboo shoots symbolic of strong legs.

Much artistry also went into the colouring of the *mee koo* (绵龟), one of them many kinds of steamed bread which are Chinese. These *mee koo* are coloured red and made from a sweetened leavened dough shaped into figures of eight. Red food colouring is then carefully applied either with a piece of cotton material or cotton-wool. A pile of these cakes, the higher the more significant the offering, makes a colourful and common sight at many Chinese festivals. Like the steamed egg cake, the *mee koo* are made or bought for most Chinese festivals. They are served during both the happy and sad occasions. When steamed, the *mee koo*, like the egg sponge, are light and spongy with a pink skin. Those made from unsweetened dough can be eaten with *kaya* or egg jam. The more skilful the kneading, the fluffier and lighter the dough, being more holey and of course, the more delicious the bread, whether sweetened or not.

A different type of unsweetened dough or pastry is used to make the outer skin wrappings for *bao* (饱) or *mantou* which are buns with a variety of different sweet or savoury fillings. These fillings can either be sweet ground peanuts, pork and egg, *char siew* or roasted lean pork, sesame paste, lotus paste, egg jam or even sweetened grated desiccated coconut. The *bao* are white in colour but those which are offered during festivals have usually each a dab of red food colouring. Those most used for festivals are shaped like peaches with sweet peanut fillings. Only sweet fillings are used for the *bao* which are part of the offerings during Chinese festivals because salty or *kiam* (咸) describes stinginess and is also an adjective for a difficult and hard life, one which is full of toil or bad fortune. Being peasants, many of the Chinese knew about toil and sweat and its salty taste.

There are small and large varieties of *bao*. Usually, the smaller ones are used for religious food offerings. The large *bao* is a feast in itself, being traditionally filled with lean slices of pork and bamboo shoot heaped one on top of the other in a mound within which are concealed pieces of chicken and pig's liver, slivers of Chinese mushrooms, a quarter of an egg and Chinese sausage.

Peaches symbolise longevity and the ones into which cakes like the *bao*, are shaped, are called fairy peaches after those that are according to Chinese mythology supposed to be eaten by the heavenly deities for immortality. Although they are sometimes referred to as long-life buns this has nothing to do with how long the buns last if they are left uneaten but rather their symbolic significance of longevity. These peaches are made from an unsweetened but leavened dough, rather like the pastry used for *bao* skin wrappings. The pastry peaches are left white but with a delicate sprinkling of fine red dots at the top end cleft where the stem of the fruit is supposed to be. Some dough which is coloured green is then used to shape the leaves on each bun before steaming. In appearance, these pastries are made to look as much as real peaches as possible.

The sweetened bread dough used to make *mee koo* is also shaped into tortoises and coloured red with food dye for festivals. Red beans are used for the eyes and this sweet bread is very popular among the children during celebrations. In particular, the tortoises were made together with *mee koo* during the festival of the ninth god, *kee ong yah* (九皇爷) or the Double Ninth Festival. This festival commemorates the birthday of a god which falls on the ninth day of the ninth lunar month. Like the peaches, the tortoises symbolise longevity and these that are made out of dough add much colour to the food offerings of Chinese festivals. The tortoise is one of the four fabulous animals in Chinese mythology. Chinese characters with auspicious meanings which are moulded from dough and coloured gaily in yellows and greens, are often added to the top of the pastry tortoises and the *mee koo.*

An entirely different type of dough is used to make the *moh haw kueh* (望翁粿) which is seen most often during the Hungry Ghosts' Festival and *Phor Tor* (普渡) celebrations. This is a festival which is especially important to the businessmen, tradesmen and also craftsmen. Some confectioners refer to this type of cake by the trade name of laughing cakes (笑粿). This is probably because of the fissures at the top of the cakes which resemble wide grins or smiles. The dough which is used to make these cakes is different because it is sweetened with a finer texture and the cakes are also slightly sticky. Stacks of the cakes mark the offerings of each group of tradespeople. Different trades made their offerings on different days, so the butchers would be followed by the green-grocers and so forth. White with colourful dabs of pink and yellow, these cakes are like the egg sponge, popular because when the dough rises during steaming, fissures will appear on the tops of the cakes and these also symbolise prosperity and luck. Pastry cooks who know the art of making these cakes are hard to find especially in places such as Singapore; and many bakeries have long stopped offering them for sale.

Sweet and also usually a bright shocking pink (or white with dabs of red on the top) is another Chinese pastry offering called *huat kueh* (发粿). The name of the cake means literally "prosperity cake". These cakes are steamed and made from rice flour. They have a spongy consistency and are also slightly sticky. When they are steamed, fissures will also appear on the surface, symbolising luck and prosperity.

Although they may look quite similar, the *huat kueh* are different in consistency and taste from the cakes which are called steamed rice bowl or cup cakes (碗扰糕). They are also left white or coloured pink and brown. Like the egg cakes or sponges, the fissures on the tops of these cup cakes like those on the *huat kueh* which appear after steaming, also signify the arrival of good luck. Although they are steamed, their consistency is not at all like that of the sponges or sweet bread, being more delicate in texture. The difference in the taste and texture is due to the cake mix which uses rice flour rather than wheat flour.

3. Food For *Man Yue* And Birthdays

The term *man yue* or the baby's full month after delivery is used for want of a better word. This occasion is actually the celebration of the one-month birthdays of babies. It is still an occasion for informing friends about the arrival of the baby in case they have yet to hear about it. In the past, when the villages of the Chinese people were far and scattered, these birthday celebrations would provide the occasions for informing relatives and friends about the new babies in the household. It was the custom then to inform the parents of the mother of the newborn baby of the joyful event by sending them nine red eggs. Today, it is still the practice among some Chinese communities to load the red eggs, cakes and rice at the back of the car and distribute them to both relatives and friends after the baby's first month.

Young people would not normally celebrate their birthdays otherwise. Generally, only parents and parents-in-law or the elderly members of the family who are fifty years of age or older, would celebrate birthdays. Of course, all has changed and children's birthday parties are very popular among urban Chinese families today.

The *ang koo kueh* (红龟粿), cakes of glutinous rice skins with mung bean paste or groundnut meal fillings, were the gifts of food which used to announce the baby's gender. Today, modern telecommunications have dispensed with this need. These cakes are so named because of their red skins which can be attributed to their popular use as an offering during Chinese festivals. Generally the shape of tortoise shells, the *ang koo kueh* were also shaped into peaches (桃) to announce the birth of girls and those smooth round ones (园园) the birth of boys. The more common variety found in modern bakeries and confectioneries today are the *ang koo kueh* which are shaped like tortoise shells.

This preference for red food colouring does not mean that the Chinese did not accept foods of other colours. Their partiality for good food and perhaps economic necessity may account for the inclusion of even black-coloured food in their diets. Although usually not offered during religious festivals because of its greyish hue, the *aw chow koo* (乌草糕) is almost similar to and as good as the *ang koo kueh*. Literally translated , the name means "black grass cake". It is much more fragrant because of the oat stalks *beh tiao* (麦禾) which are used to flavour the rice-powder pastry used for the skins. The oat stalks are usually found in the fields in China and it actually gives the skin its greyish tone and mottled appearance. In the past, we were usually treated to these cakes after relatives had returned from their China trips to visit relatives and the old village. Local commercial versions of this confectionery may not taste quite the same. Their skins are more likely to have been flavoured with yam rather than oat stalks.

To add to the colour of the baby's one-month birthday offerings, turmeric rice and chicken curry, all golden and bright yellow, are often given together with hard-boiled eggs dyed red. Eggs symbolise life and energy on this occasion (Lee Siow Mong in *Spectrum of Chinese Culture*). The inclusion of the chicken curry and turmeric rice also illustrates the eclecticism of the Chinese especially in the choice of their food. Kiang Kang-Hu described a time when red eggs would be sent to relatives and family

friends to announce a birth with odd numbers of eggs to
indicate a boy and even numbers a girl (*Chinese Civilisation: An Introduction to Sinology*). The pronunciation of
the word "egg" in Chinese, *tan* (蛋), sounds like the word
meaning courage (胆) and also the gall, which is regarded
as the seat of courage.

It is often the accepted gesture for recipients of these
offerings to respond with gifts of fine rice vermicelli and
eggs together with a *hong bao* for luck. Sometimes, instead of saffron rice, a more native Chinese dish which is
offered is steamed rice, *yeep peeng* (蒸饭), with groundnuts, slivers of Chinese mushrooms, lots of shallots and
spring onions, dried shrimps and preserved Chinese cabbage (包菜). A less costly version of this kind of rice is
what can literally be called "oil rice", which is glutinous
rice which has been lightly fried in oil with spring onions
and then steamed with groundnuts and dried shrimps.

Other Birthday Food Offerings

Fine vermicelli in a soup with eggs and good things
like pork, mushrooms, Chinese spinach, liver and kidney
is a favourite on festive days to celebrate major events
like birthdays, breakfast on the first day of the Chinese
lunar new year and as a dish to welcome guests of honour
and honoured friends who may not have been seen for a
while. Traditionally, a Chinese does not celebrate birthdays after the first anniversary of his birth. At most, a
person would have two eggs cooked with vermicelli and
sugar on each birthday thereafter (Lee Siow Mong in
Spectrum of Chinese Culture). Unlike the other types of

noodles which are usually served in large quantities, this fine vermicelli is often served in individual bowls, one for each guest. Cooked with just the right amount of seasoning and chicken soup, this fine rice vermicelli combination is a favourite with other Chinese food like hot roast pork, washed down with Chinese tea.

A roast pig is a popular offering not only because of the reddish tint of the skin but also the importance of pork in the Chinese diet. For Hokkien families, the offering of a roast pig is still an important annual event which is necessary in order to solicit heavenly blessing for the entire household. Usually the sons in the household chip in to pay for the roast pig. Roast pork is also popular with other food offerings during Chinese festivals like the sweetened *mee koo* (绵龟) or *huat kueh* (发粿), with Chinese tea or wine to drink. It is still the practice among the Chinese to share the roast pig which has been a religious offering with friends and relatives. Pieces of roast pork are usually distributed with the sweet bread *mee koo* the day after the religious festival.

Eggs are essential to occasions like birthdays, christenings and Chinese lunar new year festival celebrations on the first and ninth days not only because they are symbolic of birth and a new beginning but also because they are a versatile food ingredient. They are used in various steamed dishes and are also used as skin wrappings for dumplings and egg rolls. An egg mixture is used to create a skin in which chopped pork seasoned with spring onions, is wrapped. These dumplings are then cooked in a sweet and sour sauce seasoned with large onions and chillies.

Noodles have always signified longevity, which is why they are usually included in birthday celebrations, as the last dish during banquets and also in the final stage of steamed boat dinners that are organised to celebrate family reunions. Reportedly, noodles were invented as early as the Han period of Chinese history (206 BC - 220 AD), at about the same time as *doufu*. Birthday *mee* is actually a dish prepared from fresh yellow flour noodles to celebrate birthdays. The *mee* is made from flour and is first cooked in boiling water. A sauce made from pork, shrimps, liver and vegetables is then poured over the noodles. Red chillies and fried shallots are used to garnish the dish which is usually served during birthday celebrations. Noodles are of course, popular because they are inexpensive and extremely versatile as they can be prepared in a variety of ways. Most types of noodles can be quite tasty fried with only bean sprouts and soya sauce. Noodles can be used to prepare quick and substantive meals. They can also be added to left-over soups.

There are numerous varieties of Chinese noodles. Each dialect group has its own favourite type. For example, Hokkien *mee* (福建面) is well-known as is the Teochew *mee pok* (面薄) and the Cantonese *sow aw fun* (沙河粉). As observed earlier, the noodles are generally long and are usually made from either wheat or rice flour. The colours of the noodles range from white to various shades of yellow. Hokkien *mee* is a soup made from pork spare-ribs in which fresh round yellow noodles are cooked. Prawns, slices of lean pork and fish cake, *kang kong* (a local vegetable, 饗菜) and bean sprouts are then added to the dish. *Mee pok* is made from a flat yellow noodle which is sold in dried form. The noodles are cooked in boiling water and then laved in a piquant sauce made from chilli and bean paste with mince meat. Fishballs are then added to the dish. The Cantonese *wan ton mee* (云吞面) is prepared in a similar fashion but tossed in a sauce made from soya sauce, to which thin slivers of barbecued pork, chicken and Chinese mushrooms as well as *choy sum* (菜心) or Chinese spinach are added. For this dish, the noodles used are usually freshly made and are round and golden brown in colour. There is also a soup version of the *wan ton mee*. The *sow aw fun* (沙河粉) is a flat white noodle which is also freshly made and served tossed up in a sauce or in a soup. A broader version of this noodle is known as the *kway teow* (粿条) which can either be cooked in a soup or fried. It is made from rice flour. When cooked in a soup, fishballs, pieces of chicken and fish cake together with bean sprouts are usually added. There are different ways of preparing fried *kway teow*. The simplest is to fry it with dark soya sauce, eggs, bean sprouts, shrimps and sometimes, cockles. Sometimes it is prepared with slices of beef and bean sprouts. Other times it can be fried with slices of barbecued pork and fish cake, Chinese spinach or *choy sum* and fishballs.

For certain varieties of noodles like *mee*, there are both dried and fresh versions. A unique dried version is the egg noodle, a noodle which derives its golden yellow colouring from eggs. Others like *bee hoon* (米粉), a noodle which is white in colour, are usually available in a dried form. Like the other types of noodles, there is a variety of *bee hoon* ranging from the fine type to that which is very thick and round. All the different varieties can be fried or cooked in soups. A very hearty but unpretentious dish called *bak ki bee hoon* is prepared from *bee hoon* in a soup made from pork dumplings. The way of preparing these dumplings is an ingenious method of increasing the bulk of the pieces of pork and at the same time, keeping the pork tender. Each piece of pork is dipped in a batter made from either tapioca or corn flour.

Another type of dried noodle which looks like *kway teow* is known by the Hokkien name of *chiam* (豆纤). The *chiam* is made from bean flour which accounts for its different consistency. It is heavier and starchier than *kway teow* and is used in soups made from pork, dried shrimps and *choy sum*.

An equally unusual type of noodle is the so-called glass vermicelli or *tung hoon* (冬粉). Sometimes the noodle is referred to as cellophane or pea-starch noodle. The noodle, which is made from peas, is transparent and looks like rice vermicelli, being very fine. Its consistency, however, is not as soft as that of the rice vermicelli since it is more chewy. The noodle is added to soups where it could be mistaken for bird's nest. It can also be fried and eaten as a dish with rice. One of these dishes has the intriguing name of "aunt marrying her daughter off" and is prepared from the vermicelli which is fried with the vegetable known as the hairy gourd and dried shrimps. The *tung hoon* is also popular with vegetarians and is a common food offering during the *kee ong yah* festival when Chinese worshippers of this deity observe a week-long vegetarian diet.

4. Ching Ming Festival Food Offerings

We have always eaten *po piah* (薄饼) during Ching Ming (First Feast of the Dead). Other Chinese in the past have apparently eaten painted boiled eggs (Richard Wilhelm in *The Soul of China*). The period is not only a festival but also a section of the seasons in China when the weather would be clear and bright (Lee Siow Mong in *The Spectrum of Chinese Culture*). Apparently, the Chinese of today often confuse the festival with the Cold Meal Festival which falls on the day before. More likely it has less to do with confusing the festivals than the practicality of the Chinese who have probably decided to celebrate both together since the Ching Ming festival lasts for a week. The Ching Ming period is when the family remembers the generations before. Time is set for visits to the grave sites or columbariums and making offerings particularly of the things which the persons had like when they were alive. Chinese families might have opted to eat *po piah* on the day because it was the fastest way to feed a large family although there are several stories about the origins of this festival which suggest the contrary.

One is that Ching Ming commemorates the day when a patriot of the Chou Dynasty chose to die rather than accept his Sovereign Lord Tsin's gratitude for feeding him when the ruler was starving (Juliet Bredon and Igor Mitrophanow in *The Moon Year - A Record of Chinese Customs and Festivals*, 1927). The patriot had accompanied his lord on a journey. Misfortune befell them and food supplies ran out. To feed his lord, the patriot cut off a piece of his own flesh. One version of the tale has it that this patriot repeatedly refused his lord's invitation to leave his mother in the mountains in order to accept an official position in the capital city. Another version was that the lord forgot this faithful follower during the distribution of honours when he reascended the throne, whereupon, the follower retired to the mountain forest with his mother. There the lord's emissaries sent to look for him eventually failed to find him. The lord's over-zealous emissaries burnt the mountain to get the patriot to leave but tragically, both he and his mother were found burnt to death instead. Since then, the lord has decreed that on the anniversary of that fateful day no fire should be lit. This meant that only cold dishes and food prepared the day before could be served, as a sign of remembrance.

Still another version of the story, which is in Lee Siow Mong's book *The Spectrum of Chinese Culture*, has it that the king of the state of Jin (晋), Jin Wen Kong (晋文公), had to flee from his state due to civil unrest. His friend, Jie Zhi-zhui (介子推) followed him for seventeen of his nineteen years of wandering. When the king was reinstated, his friend Jie refused the offer of a high official post because he found officialdom and politics futile. He retired to the hills, Mian Shan (绵山), where he preferred to remain, turning down repeated requests from his king. The king, in a fit of frustration, set fire to the woods to try and force Jie out. Tragically, both he and his mother were found burnt to death, clinging to a tree. A remorseful king decreed that no fire was to be lit in homes on the anniversary of that day, giving rise to the Cold Meal Festival, the day before Ching Ming.

A more down-to-earth version was that food like *po piah* could be prepared and packed when the family travelled up to the hills where the dead they were paying respects to would usually be buried. That way *po piah* with their meat and vegetable fillings served as nutritious meals for large families taking a break from cleaning the graves or before setting out for home.

Everyone could fix their own *po piah* the way they like them best, putting all the ingredients onto each pancake and then rolling them up. They could be long and just right or short and fat, stuffed full of different types of food ranging from shrimps, crab meat, radish and carrot salad with cuttlefish, lettuce, bean sprouts, french beans to egg omelette sliced thinly and various types of bean and chilli sauces. The left-over *po piah* can also be deep-fried, minus the bean and chilli sauces. These deep-fried *po piah* are then served with a variety of sauces.

5. Moon-Cakes And The Moon-Cake Festival

The moon-cake festival is celebrated more by young people and children. There have been different ways of celebrating this festival. In the 1950s, young men and women would gather in parks and gardens in the town to sing and eat under the full moon. There would be moonlight parties (月光会) in most houses when families would take their food out into the verandahs and gardens to watch the full moon while they ate. Children would be carrying lanterns on that night, forming long lines of bobbing lights and the village would be bright with their merrymaking as they wound their way in and out between the homes.

Moon-cakes originated in the Yuan dynasty. According to historical records, the people were unhappy and oppressed under the tyrannical rule of the emperor. A peasant leader, Zhu Yuang Zhang, organised a revolution on the day of the mid-autumn festival. He aroused support among the people by passing secret messages which were hidden in moon-cakes. Together, they successfully rebelled against their Mongol rulers and later founded the Ming dynasty. The festival therefore commemorates the overthrow of Mongolian rule by the Han Chinese.

The moon-cake festival probably began as a harvest festival. Harvesting season was celebrated by the Chinese farmers as it was an occasion for thanksgiving especially when the harvest was plentiful. It was also a season signifying the end of the year's toil in the fields before the new year's round of planting and labouring.

The moon-cake festival has also been linked to the legend of Chang-E, the lady in the moon, worshipped especially by the Cantonese. Following Chinese mythology, Chang-E was the wife of the strong archer, Hou Yi, who saved the earth from the scorching heat of ten suns which once appeared together. Hou Yi, so the legend goes, shot down nine of these suns. He stole the elixir of life but to save the earth from his tyranny, his wife drank it and found herself floating to the moon. The Chinese have since prayed to her during the mid-Autumn festival and many claim to see her shadow flitting about on the moon during this festival. Another version of the legend has it that one of the retainers of Hou Yi was seeking to steal the elixir when he came upon Chang-E playing with it. Chang-E was so frightened by the retainer's threats to make her surrender the elixir, she swallowed it and flew to the moon.

While the origins of moon-cakes are well-known, less so are the varieties which abound because each dialect groups fixes theirs differently, just as they have different types of rice dumplings. The common Cantonese variety has either lotus seed or bean paste filling which are varying shades of beige, brown and black. Care has to be taken to ensure that only the young and tender lotus seeds are used. The use of older seeds gives the filling a bitter undertaste. The filling can be plain, made with one or more salted ducks' egg yolks or mixed with melon seeds. There is a variety, the *kum toy* which is chiefly a mix of nuts like almonds embedded in a sticky sweet jelly with little bits of fat.

The skins of the moon-cakes which are used to wrap the sweet fillings vary in kind. They range from those made of flour to others which are made of glutinous rice and flaky pastry. The glutinous rice skin or more fancifully called, snow skin, is actually the confectionery which is called *kiat hong ko* (吉祥粿). Ordinarily, the *kiat hong ko* is made into little squares which are then dusted with rice flour and wrapped in white paper. They are actually a Chinese-style Turkish delight. Several versions of the *kiat hong ko* are currently available in the old-style Chinese biscuit shops and bakeries. The modern versions are often coloured pink and pastel green with dull red decorations. Another modern innovation is banana-flavoured *kiat hong ko*. The Cantonese have their own version of this delightful sweet, which is slightly stickier and are often commercially produced.

The Teochew moon-cakes have flaky biscuit skins and unlike the Cantonese moon-cakes because they are usually round and slightly flatter. There are moon-cakes with white skins and others with red skins. The Chao Zhao moon-cakes usually have yam and egg fillings and lard in the "melt-in-the-mouth" skins. Moon-cakes are usually round in shape, like the moon. Some are eaten by the Cantonese all the year round. They are also popular as wedding biscuits among the Cantonese.

In addition, there are plain moon-cakes made out of the same dough used for wrapping those with fillings but the dough is sweetened and then either moulded or handcrafted into various animal shapes like fishes, crabs and birds or the deities of Prosperity, Happiness and Longevity (Hock Lock Siew). The pig is a favourite and each is packed into a little basket made to resemble the big one in which a pig is sent to the market for sale. These cakes are enormously popular with children.

Some people bake the moon-cakes themselves as a symbolic act, in remembrance of the deliverance of their ancestors from oppressors. In the past, if the people could afford it, they would stuff the moon-cakes they were making with bits of lard, spices, melon seeds, almonds, orange peel and sugar (Juliet Bredon and Igor Mitrophanow in *The Moon Year — A Record of Chinese Customs and Festivals*). Confectioners of old would present the moon-cakes to the poor in the cities of China while in the villages moon-cake societies were often formed with the purpose of collecting donations with which to buy every family moon-cakes for the festival. The poor of the village would usually donate a few coppers a time to the baker who would be allowed to use the capital until the festival when he would have to distribute moon-cakes to everyone in the village.

6. The Food Of Chinese Lunar New Year

The biscuits and cakes which are symbolic and served or presented as gifts during the Chinese lunar new year have been discussed. More of the food which is used as religious offerings will be discussed in subsequent sections of the book as this festive occasion is celebrated on a lavish scale meant to culminate the labour and harvests of the old year while welcoming the new year with hopes of better fortune and plenty for the family. Indeed, it is the occasion when it would appear that all the effort of each Chinese family is concentrated on showing friends and kin alike the abundance of food and goodwill in the household. The name used to refer to the Chinese reunion dinner means "surrounding the pot". This also referred to the practice of having a steamboat meal during the reunion which used to be ideal for warming the family as well as eating and cooking together the food symbolic of the abundance of the land, sea and sky. The practice has not been popular in the many tropical countries where the Chinese have settled.

Some of the dishes specifically served up during Chinese lunar new year celebrations will be discussed in this section. Fish symbolises abundance because of the similarity of its Chinese character to the word which means abundance. It has therefore to be served during the festive meal. A fish dish which is most commonly known is the *yee sang* or *fa cai yu sheng*, a raw fish dish consisting of a salad made up usually of some 15 vegetables and other ingredients, is eaten on the seventh day of the lunar new year. This dish is a must for the Cantonese and the Teochew, especially the businessmen, as it is supposed to bring a lifetime of wealth and prosperity. However, the practice is limited more to the Chinese in Malaysia and Singapore as the Cantonese in Hong Kong do not eat the dish specifically during the lunar new year festivities. They eat raw fish at other times too.

Eaten on the seventh day of the lunar new year, a day known as "people's day", the *yu* or fish symbolises abundance and prosperity and the *yu sheng* is evocative of liveliness. In Cantonese, *sheng* conjures up the picture of business expansion or prosperity. Before the dish is eaten, the diners go through the act of *lo hei* or tossing up good fortune, that is, tossing the raw fish and salad and thoroughly mixing the ingredients. Early versions of the dish comprised thinly sliced raw fish, fresh vegetables with white vinegar, sugar, salt and whole peppercorns. The dish is now more elaborate. The Qing dynasty version comprised just raw fish sprinkled with oil. One version of the *yu sheng* served today includes the raw fish with an array of preserved melon strips, sweetened lime strips, preserved cucumber strips, white sour ginger strips, red sweetened ginger strips, preserved leek strips, preserved mixed melon strips, sweetened Buddha hand fruit strips, mashed peanuts and fried sesame. The sauce includes lemon sauce, plum sauce and paste to which are added jellyfish, *pok chui* or deep fried crackers, pepper powder, cinnamon powder and China rice vinegar. Other ingredients include green radish, peanut oil, pine nuts, carrots, pomelo, sweet potato, sweet turnip, spring onion, shredded ginger, Chinese parsley and shredded red chilli. The Teochew-style *yu sheng* contains more fish with less vegetables and is eaten with a plum sauce dip.

There are other dishes which symbolise prosperity. One goes by the Cantonese name of *kong poh hei* which combines sea snails, broccoli and carrot fried in oyster sauce and is meant to make the diner look prosperous (*New Straits Times*, 22 January 1990). Another is the *ho pau moon yao moon* which is steamed chicken wrapped in lotus leaves. It is meant to symbolise full wallets. Finally, the *ho see chai chai lai*, which is minced oyster cooked with lettuce, is a dish meant to bring all the good things in life.

For the Teochew families especially, the use of honey pea pods in lunar new year dishes symbolises a good start to the year as the vegetable has a sweet taste. Dishes prepared with scallops and broccoli represent *fu qui hua kai* or the blossoming of luck and fortune. Food like abalone, sea cucumbers or urchins and Chinese mushrooms symbolise smooth progress in business and work, *yi peng wan li*.

The food prepared for the lunar new year meals by the northern Chinese such as those from Tianjin, are also symbolic and signify the aspirations and hopes of the diners. Boiled dumplings or *jiaozi* are eaten on the first day of the lunar new year because when cooked they look like gold and therefore signify wealth. On the second day, *laomian*, noodles tossed in heavy syrup, are eaten; these symbolise longevity. A flat round dumpling, *hezi*, which represents the wheel of fortune, must be served on the third day. It is gaily coloured. Usually three colours are used as the Chinese character for "three" sounds like the word "rise" which connotes prosperity, progress and all things good (*Straits Times*, 20 January

1990). Orange is used because it is the colour nearest to gold and green like jade.

Cantonese dishes for the lunar new year include fish porridge and steamed buns or *mantou*. The sound of the name of this confectionery is similar to that meaning bountiful food.

PART TWO

FOOD OF SYMBOLIC SIGNIFICANCE

7. Rice And Other Cereals Of Symbolic Significance

There is more to rice than frying. Rice, especially to the Chinese whose ancestors hail from southern mainland China, is a staple and its abundance is a symbol of prosperity and life. Rice in abundance is therefore a source of happiness and hence, a cause for celebration. Until today, the elderly Chinese people prefer their rice *congee* thick and cooked with lots of rice because watery *congee* necessarily means hard times and rice rationing in order to stretch available supplies of rice. Chinese businessmen still comment on their daily business in terms of whether they are to dine on *congee* (business is bad) or white rice (times are good). When an extra bowl of rice is inadvertently cooked, it foretells the arrival of an unexpected guest.

Glutinous rice and rice flour tend to be less well-regarded because they are reputedly capable of bloating up the stomach and sinking to the bottom of it like a deadweight. Nonetheless, they are a common ingredient in Chinese cakes and especially those of *peranakan* origin. It is no wonder, therefore, that rice and dishes made from rice and rice flour figure prominently in many Chinese festivals and nearly all celebrations. Some dialect groups arrange for rice to be thrown or scattered at weddings, usually around the time the bridegroom arrives to fetch his bride home.

In his 1864 book on the *Social Life of the Chinese*, Reverend Justus Doolittle explained that rice used to play an even more important part in Chinese weddings. Five bunches of boiled rice, each consisting of five bundles

which were conical in shape and tied with leaves and red
strings, would be suspended from the frame used for the
curtain of the bridal bed. One of the bunches would be
bigger and was referred to as the "mother" while the
others were called the "children". Five yams or taros, one
large and four small, would also be placed beneath the
bed. In the centre of the bed would be placed a wooden
vessel half-filled with rice. A piece of red paper was then
placed over the vessel on which were offered various
items including food like five kinds of dried fruits and a
mandarin orange. These offerings of food and other ar-
ticles were meant to secure prosperity for the married
couple especially the bearing of children in their family
in successive generations.

A huge eight-sided bowl (八角碗) of rice grains is still a
common religious offering on festive occasions. There
were records of a feast of ancient origin celebrated on the
eighth day of the twelfth lunar month on the morning
of which a thick porridge was prepared from old rice
stored in the granaries, whole grains of several kinds,
beans, nuts, fruits and four varieties of sugar. The eighth
day of the twelfth lunar month is known as 腊八. (Henry
Dore in *Researches into Chinese Superstitions*). There was
the custom of making the porridge from five kinds of
grains — rice, millet, wheat, pulse and hemp — and
vegetables, to which were added a variety of fruits —
earth nuts, chestnuts, dates and in some places, dates
and water caltrops, seeds of medlar and the trumpet
creeper. These ingredients were boiled into a thick porridge known as the *la pa chuh* (腊八粥). The Buddhists had
their own version of this porridge which was made from
seven precious ingredients and five tastes. They would

send the porridge, *tsih-pao wu-wei-chuh* (七宝五味粥), to benefactors.

According to Juliet Bredon and Igor Mitrophanow in their 1927 publication of *The Moon Year — A Record of Chinese Customs and Festivals*, the legend concerning the origins of the porridge dish involved the poor mother of an unfilial son who was driven to beg for food from her neighbours. One neighbour gave her a handful of grains, another a tray of fruits and the third a bowl of beans. The dish she cooked with the ingredients has been eaten since by the Chinese as a symbol of brotherhood. The two authors, Bredon and Mitrophanow, have also recorded the presentation of gifts of soups made from white cabbage to friends during the twelfth lunar month. From the taste of the cabbage, whether sweet or sour, friends were then able to foretell whether good or evil fortune awaited them.

The eating of round balls of sweetened rice during wedding celebrations in China has symbolic significance as it means the hope for a life of unbroken harmony for the couple (Alasdair Clayre in *Heart of the Dragon*). During the festival to celebrate the ninth day of the Chinese lunar new year, the "centrepieces", taking pride of place on the altar tables, are pink-coloured sugar sculptures (糖塔) placed in beds of rice grains in containers lined with red paper. The centre of the three sculptures is a pagoda and this is flanked by a lion and a dragon. After the festival, these sugar sculptures are usually melted down and used to sweeten drinks like barley water, our local equivalent of pink lemonade, and also to make *agar-agar*, the hard jelly-like dessert which is made by dissolving the transparent, dried *agar-agar* strips in boiling water and then allowing it to set.

Besides birthday rice (糯米饼) which is made from glutinous rice steamed with groundnuts, mushrooms and dried shrimps, glutinous rice is also used to make puddings called *bee ko* (米糕). These puddings are made from glorious mixes of glutinous rice, coconut milk and sugar, lightly flavoured with *pandan* and then steamed. They are usually decorated with preserved red dates and are often used as offerings in festivals. Like the *mee koo*, these puddings are also good when eaten with roast pork as they are quite often offered together during a festival.

Black glutinous rice, variously known as *pulut hitam* or *obee boey* (黑糯米粥), are cooked with dried longans and sweetened and is a favourite dessert served to women during the month of confinement after delivery. A local contribution is the addition of coconut *santan* for extra flavour and fragrance. The colour of the dish is a deep maroon rather than black, as the name suggests.

Glutinous rice flour is also used to make the skin of the steamed buns *cai bao* (菜饱). The filling is made of shredded radish, carrots and pork with ground peanuts. Some skill is required in steaming so that the *bao* is cooked just right with the ground peanuts looking as if they have just been added to the filling. A dab of red on each steamed *bao* completes the offering on a festive occasion. These buns are served steamed on little round pieces of banana leaf or they can be steamed and then lightly fried till the outside is crispy before serving. Similarly, *ang koo kueh* can be served fried with crispy skins.

Glutinous rice is also used to make the Chinese lunar new year cake known as the *ti kueh* (sweet cake) or *nien*

Peanut brittle and *kong t'ng* (middle)

Por Tor festivities

Muay lau and *lau huay* (front)

Making *yu-tiao*

Steamed egg cake   Mee koo

Bee chiang, huat kueh and *mee koo*

Bowl cakes

"Peach" buns

1 Pc =.
2 Pcs = 50¢
4 Pcs = 4.00

1 Pc
40¢

Aw Chow koo and *ang koo kueh*

Ingredients for making *po piah*

Sugar Sculptures

Dried bean-curd sheets

Festive offering of *bee ko* and eggs

A tidbits stall

Dried cuttlefish

Bao

Tung yuan

Fine rice vermicelli

Goh kor giok chye

gao (年糕). The glutinous nature of the cake symbolises family unity and togetherness or sticking together through thick and thin. Its Chinese name signifies yearly increases and achievements. A story which has been passed down through the generations was that *nien gao* or honey was offered to deities like the kitchen god in order to make it more difficult for the god to report adverse things about the family during his annual trip to Heaven. These cakes are made from mixtures of glutinous rice and sugar. The caramelising of the sugar gives the cakes a rich golden brown colour after they have been steamed. Before steaming, the cake mixture is poured into individual baskets or tins lined with banana leaves. A good year for the housewives making the cakes are steamed cakes with perfectly smooth surfaces. Mottling is usually taken to be a bad omen. After the Chinese lunar new year celebrations, these cakes are usually preserved by drying them in the sun. They are eaten in several ways as breakfast food and also as snacks. One way is to cut the cake into slices and steam them. The reconstituted cake is then either eaten plain or dipped in fresh grated coconut, a local adaptation. Small children usually eat theirs plain and like spun sugar, each wound round a chopstick. Another way of eating the cake is to sandwich slices of them in between pieces of yam or sweet potato, dipping each sandwich into a batter prepared from rice flour and eggs and then deep-frying them. The result is a crispy snack. Sometimes it is eaten by deep-frying pieces of the cake in batter made from wheat flour and eggs. The Cantonese make it a point to eat *nien gao* on the seventh day of the lunar new year festivities, the day which is also known as "people's day".

Powdered glutinous rice is used to make bean jelly which is popular in Shanghai dishes. The jelly, so-called because it is transparent, is made from rice and water. It is then cut into cubes and added to fish dishes.

The reasons for eating rice dumplings on the fifth day in the fifth month of the Chinese lunar new year are well-known. Less well-known are the many types of rice dumplings which are available. This is the Dragon Boat Festival or the festival of the sun. The rice dumplings began as triangular cakes made of rice in the south of China and millet in the north. Each of the cakes was stuffed with a bit of sugar or candied fruit inside (Juliet Bredon and Igor Mitrophanow in *The Moon Year — A Record of Chinese Customs and Festivals*, 1927). These rice cakes bear little resemblance to the more sophisticated versions of the rice dumplings of today. There was formerly little need to be conversant with the dates of festivals in the Chinese lunar calendar to be reminded that it was time again for the celebration of the fifth day of the fifth lunar month. This was because the sight of the ingredients used in the preparation of the rice dumplings — straw, lotus, water-flag (菖蒲草) or bamboo leaves, grass strings and glutinous rice as well as the dried and preserved ingredients soaking — was a sufficient reminder of the festival at hand.

The Hokkien *ba tsung* (肉粽) is a skilfully constructed three-cornered cone or pyramid of glutinous rice steamed in bamboo leaves tied together with grass strings. The dumpling is stuffed with pieces of succulent pork, whole mushrooms and chestnuts. Another type is the *tao tsung*

(豆粽) which is almost similar to the one with pork but is studded with yellow black-eyed beans. The simpler and plainer version is the dumpling made from glutinous rice with *ki* called *ki ah tsung* (枳糕). Also steamed in bamboo or straw leaves tied together with grass strings, this dumpling goes well with braised leg of pork cooked with whole cloves of garlic, Chinese mushrooms, star anise, sticks of cinnamon and sea cucumber. The plain dumpling also tastes good with *kaya* or dipped in sugar and even caramel made from *gula melaka*.

While there is a variety of nonya dumplings, the most distinctive is the triangular piece of glutinous rice with black-eyed beans, wrapped in yellow lotus leaves which are tied up in knots in the three corners. It is usually lightly salted and eaten dipped in fine sugar. Its name defies imagination: 猪八怪. There is some reason to believe that it could be a Chinese mispronunciation of the word *ketupat*, which is also a leaf-wrapped rice cake usually eaten with *satay*.

The Cantonese and Teochew dumplings, which are a favourite with most Chinese, have everything in them. They are stuffed with pork (steamed until they melt in the mouth), mushrooms, chestnuts, dried oysters or shrimps and a salted egg yolk. The fragrance of these dumplings is heavenly, so goes the claim of many aficionados. Teochew dumplings, like the Sichuan kind, are both sweet and savoury. In the Sichuan dumpling, the savoury filling is added to a sweet red date paste. Teochew dumplings have stuffings of which half would be sweet and half savoury.

During the Dragon Boat Festival when the rice dumplings were eaten, it was also a custom to drink a small

amount of realgar (arsenic sulphide) wine
(雄黃酒) and paint the realgar on the foreheads, cheeks,
noses and ears of children to ward off poisonous creatures which were a common threat during the summer
(Lee Siow Mong in *The Spectrum of Chinese Culture*). The
five poisonous creatures were the *wu du* (五毒) or five
poisons — the centipede, scorpion, snake, lizard and
toad. The shapes of these creatures were moulded on the
tops of cakes which were then eaten, to symbolise the
neutralising of these pests. Another version of the five
poisons lists them as the viper, spider, toad, centipede
and scorpion (Henry Dore in *Researches into Chinese Superstitions*). Folklore, however, has it that the wine was
drunk in order to expose snake spirits. According to the
legend of Madam White Snake, the husband of a beautiful woman, who was actually a snake spirit, only found
out the truth after she had drunk wine during the celebration of the Dragon Boat Festival.

The Dragon Boat Festival or the Fifth Moon Festival,
celebrated on the fifth day of the fifth lunar month, had
its origins during the period of the Warring States. The
festival was actually started in remembrance of the death
of a patriot, Ju Yuan, who drowned himself that day
because his attempts at improving the condition of his
country and people could not be achieved. A weak emperor and scheming court officials who were jealous of
him prevented the fruition of his plans. The Chinese
have since thrown glutinous rice into the river to prevent
the fishes from consuming Ju Yuan's body. Dragon boat
races were held to symbolise the race across the river to
reach the patriot. During the Han dynasty, an apparition
of Ju Yuan was reportedly seen who complained that he

had not been getting any of the rice offerings because they had been eaten by sea dragons. Since then the rice has been offered in bamboo leaves tied with strings. These are the *tsung* which are still eaten today.

Rice which is ground on stone mills and mixed with *ki* water (枧水) is used to make *ki ah kueh* (枧粿). *Ki* water is a highly versatile ingredient which is also added to make the fresh yellow noodles, mee (面) and also soya bean curd and bean curd cakes. In the past, the people in China made *ki* water from a wild grass. Nowadays it is an alkaline solution made from chemicals. The rice mixture used in *ki ah kueh* is steamed in huge baskets lined with muslin and more often than not, used as a festival offering. A light golden colour when it is steamed, the *ki ah kueh* is a popular accompaniment to braised leg of pork cooked the way it has been described earlier. It is also usually eaten with *kaya* or egg jam.

Rice is also sometimes added to red and green mung bean soups to add substance. The red bean porridge used to be eaten on the twenty-fifth day of the twelfth month in the belief that it would ward off evil because the deity for epidemics was afraid of red beans (Henry Dore in *Researches into Chinese Superstitions*). In the past, *teu-fu-cha* (豆腐渣), a bean curd food, used to be added to the porridge. This red bean porridge is known as " the porridge for all folks and all mouths", *chih-teu-chuh* (赤豆粥). Nowadays the porridge is eaten without the belief that used to be attached to it. The rice certainly adds colour to these sweet soups which are now often served as desserts. Dried fruits and fruit peels are sometimes added. The tangy taste and fragrance in red bean soup comes from dried mandarin peel. Dried longans are also sometimes added to the red bean soup. So are dried lotus seeds. Extra flavour in the soup made from mung beans would be from adding *pandan* leaves or *gula melaka* and coconut milk.

Yam flavoured rice flour cakes are sometimes added to *chee cheong fun* to enhance the meal if not add substance. Pieces of steamed yam and *sung* (松) would be added to glutinous ground rice mix and then steamed. When they are served on their own, yam cakes are usually made richer. A layer of stir-fried thinly sliced pork, dried prawns, spring onions, shallots, and slivers of mushrooms is usually added to the cake before steaming. The yam cake is then garnished with red chilli and served with hot and sweet bean sauce.

Rice grains which are roast fried in a wok with ginger and shallots are used to make a rice tea. This is a popular drink for women during their confinement period after the delivery of their babies. Rice is also good for rice wine which is often used in Chinese cooking and also marinades. Witness the varieties of "drunken" dishes which are on the menus of Chinese restaurants.

A *peranakan* dish, which has been incorporated into the Chinese diet, has as one of its main ingredients, ground rice. This is flavoured with a mix of curry powder and various local herbs and serves as a savoury pudding base in which seafood such as fish cutlets, shrimps, squid and cockles are steamed in rattan basket-trays lined with banana leaves. Among Malaysian Chinese, the dish is usually known by the kind of seafood used — so if it is fish, the dish is known as fish parcel or in Chinese, fish *bao*. In Singapore there is another version which is bar-becued rather than steamed and is called *otak-otak*. The ingredients are, however, basically similar although the rice pudding base is used in smaller quantities. While the Malaysian version is wrapped in the leaves of the leprous lime plant (probably so called because of the many lumps on the limes) and banana, the Singaporean version is cooked only in banana leaves. The lime bears some resemblance to the lemons known as "Buddha's fingers" which are shaped like a half-closed hand. These lemons are usually laid out in bowls on shining grains of uncooked rice during the twelfth lunar month in preparation for the lunar new year celebrations (Juliet Bredon and Igor Mitrophanow in *The Moon-Year — A Record of Chinese Customs and Festivals*).

Other types of grains also have special significance. Bran, *fu-tze* (麩子) is the homonym of the characters which mean a rich son, *fu tze* (富子). It has therefore been used as a gift portent of progeny (Henry Dore in *Researches into Chinese Superstitions*, Volumes I-X). According to Dore, a present that was always received with pleasure during the pre-wedding rituals was seven types of grains, *ts'ih-tze-li* (七子礼), which are also portents of many children and future happiness.

8. Preserved Food And Fresh Fruits

The art of preserving food has developed among the Chinese for centuries. There is a wide array of different types of food from land, sea and sky which are preserved through drying in the sun or various methods using brine, sugar and even earth. With preservation, the Chinese have been able to widen the already large range of food varieties in their cuisine. They have produced the unique, so-called century-old eggs for example, through their skill at preservation.

Tidbits

The above label belies the rich range of preserves which are included in the classification. More appropriate is the Chinese name which literally translated means "salty-sour-sweet" (咸酸甜). These preserves provide a range of tastes actually ranging from salty to sour and sweet. They are meant to help with all manner and degree of nausea or morning sickness. There are sweet and salted Chinese olives (橄榄) as well as the ones coated in *kum cho*, a yellow powder (乾草) not unlike saffron. These olives come in an array of colours from yellow to golden brown, red, green and black. As ubiquitous and quite traditional are the preserved leeks *lar ngiao* (腌荞). They are a potent blend of tastes mixing sweetness and the tang of onions. Nutmeg is not only a popular spice but also a tidbit. There are varieties of this tidbit which are sweetened. One is soaked in sugar syrup and available in halves. Each of the halves has usually been sliced before packaging. Another variety is made from fine slivers of nutmeg tossed in sugar.

There is preserved candied lime which is sweet but there are other popular versions which are salty or sour. Preserved prunes also come in sweet, sour or salty forms as well as coated with *kum cho*. The taste of lime is used in analogy to describe a person's fortune which has been bitter and difficult in the beginning but then changes for the better, that is, a sweet ending. One hears gossips applying this sage comparison to the lives of people who have had a difficult time initially struggling to make ends meet and then subsequently amassed great wealth by a stroke of good luck or through sheer hard work.

Peaches are usually salted, however, and stained yellow because of the liquid in which they are preserved or dyed red. There is salted ginger which is also dyed a fiery red and is hot in taste. The taste of many of the preserves is generally tangy and just their mention is sufficient to make mouths water, at least among those who have been initiated into the world of Chinese tidbits. Sometimes all the three tastes — sweet, salty and sour — are provided by a single tidbit. Small brown Chinese pears are first preserved in salt which makes them salty and sourish. They are then coated in caramel rather like toffee apples.

Preserved fruits which are eaten as tidbits range from arbutus to dates. Most are dried while others are just soaked in brine. Dates, both black and red, are either dried or sweetened. There are also those coated in *kum cho*. Dried dates are much used in Chinese broths and soups especially the herbal varieties. Because of their colour, red dates are a popular offerings on festivals. The eating of red dates is believed to bring one good year after another (吃红枣年年好). On the ninth day of the Chinese lunar new year celebrations, sticks of red dates alternating with dried longans in their skins and groundnuts coated in batter are part of an important offering called the *bee chiang* (蜜将). Longans are also an important ancestral offering because they symbolise happiness and union. The fruit is round and sweet in taste. It is generally offered during the festival together with the roast pig.

Dried fruits are also the ingredients of sweets like the *ling mong* tablets (柠檬) and the haw flakes or *san sar pe* (山楂饼). Various kinds of dried peel are included as well. Mandarin peel provides a pleasant tangy aftertaste. Just as stimulating is the peel of mango.

Dried Food

Several varieties of dried fruits including red dates, winter melon (冬瓜), longans or dragon's eyes, figs and persimmons together with gingko nuts, lotus seeds and white fungus are used to make sweet teas. Winter melon is coated with sugar to preserve it and is often a sweetener in herbal teas. There is a rhyming couplet to the effect that eating longans leads to a sweet fate. Another couplet is more negative and applied to choosy people in their search for a spouse. This couplet warns them that they will only end up with rotten longans if they are too fussy. The sweet tea is normally served during the Chinese lunar new year festival. Traditionally, the tea is prepared by the daughter-in-law who offers it to her parents-in-law and husband on the morning of the first day of Chinese lunar new year. The sweet tea is drunk by all during the Chinese new year celebration because of the significance of its ingredients. Eating winter melon is believed to bring yearly prosperity. Lotus seeds are supposed to bless the family with good sons year after year (吃莲仔,年年生贵仔). Red dates, winter melon and lotus seeds are therefore popular offerings during major celebrations like the Chinese new year. Gingko nuts or the *peh kwo-tze* (百菓仔) or seeds of the maiden-hair tree are auspicious offerings because the name sounds like the characters *peh-ko-tze* (百个子) which means "numerous offspring".

The better known of the dried foods are those used as offerings especially during the various prominent and auspicious days of the Chinese lunar new year. In the past, the Chinese celebrated the ninth day of their new year as the birthday of vegetables, *tsai sheng-jeh* (菜生日).

The offerings of the dried fruits and vegetables are collectively called *goh kor giok chye* (五果六菜). Literally translated, the name means "five fruits and one vegetable", certainly a no-nonsense guide to the number of dishes required as offerings. In their 1927 book *The Moon Year — A Record of Chinese Customs and Festivals*, Juliet Bredon and Igor Mitrophanow wrote that peas and vegetables were thrown on the kitchen roof during the lunar new year celebrations to herald the departure of the kitchen god on his journey to heaven. These vegetable offerings were meant to bring luck to cattle and ensure plentiful fodder in the year to come.

Huat chai (发菜), a seaweed, is commonly known to symbolise luck and prosperity. Commonly, other festival offerings include black woodears fungus or *bok bee* (木耳), lily flowers or *kim am cai* (金针菜), *mui cai* (梅菜), *char cai* (榨菜), *chee cai* (紫菜) and groundnuts. The black fungus symbolises intelligence because it resembles human ears (Evelyn Lip in *Notes on Things Chinese*). The white fungus which grows at the roots of pine trees in China is highly regarded as a symbol of immortality. It is called the fungus of longevity.

Dishes in which these dried foods are used as ingredients are just as interesting. The dried lily flowers can be knotted and then added as a vegetable to broths and braised leg of pork. They are useful garnishes in dishes of stir-fried vegetables, adding colour and variety. This dried vegetable also adds a certain piquancy to broths and other dishes.

If the cook had run out of fresh greens for soups and vegetable dishes during those times before the Chinese learned about other ways of preserving food like canning and freezing, it was possible to save the day with dried foods and preserved vegetables like the spicy *char cai*. The vegetable is a flavoursome addition to soups made of spare-ribs, pork or chicken stock and bones.

Dried food which is popular among the Chinese include several varieties of seafood. The more inexpensive are dried shrimps and cuttlefish. Dried cuttlefish is often found among religious offerings. Being a type of fish, it symbolises the bounty of the sea and families offering it together with vegetables and meat can say that they have offered meals with everything — meat, fish and vegetables. In the past, fish which had been freshly caught

would not have been readily available to peasant families living in the inland parts of China and who were
chiefly farmers.

Cuttlefish like dried shrimps is also added to many
Chinese dishes. The more expensive types of dried
seafoods are dried scallops, abalones and oysters. These
sea creatures are popular partly because they resemble
various forms of Chinese money. When available they
are also added to several types of dishes. Dried scallops
and oysters are ingredients used in stir-fried vegetable
dishes. Oysters are added to braised pork dishes and even
in Cantonese rice dumplings.

Fresh Fruits

While dried fruits are usually offered, fresh fruits are
preferred during festive occasions such as Chinese new
year. Five types of fruits form part of the food offerings
during the moon-cake or harvest festival which falls on
the fifteenth day of the eighth lunar month. During the
Chinese lunar new year festival, fresh fruits symbolise a
new beginning.

The pomelo, mandarin, lime, banana, pineapple and
water melon are often seen as festival offerings. Pomegranates embody the hope for many children since the
fruit has many seeds. The fruit is not native to China and
originated from Central Asia sometime in the beginning
of the Christian era. A pre-wedding ritual , no longer
practised, has been described by Henry Dore in *Researches
into Chinese Superstitions*, Volumes I-X. After fixing the
day of marriage, the bridegroom sends presents to the

bride's family in a red box. These include pomegranates, *shih-liu* (石榴), which auger numerous progeny. Fruits contain a large number of seeds, *tze* (仔), and the Chinese character for this word has a similar sound to the one meaning "children", *tze* (子). Jujubes or dates formed part of the pre-nuptial gift because their name *tsao-tze* (枣仔) is pronounced in the same manner as *tsao-tze* (早子) which means "have children quickly". Date soup is still drunk in China during wedding celebrations because of the symbolic significance of dates (Alasdair Clayre in *Heart of the Dragon*).

Similarly, chestnuts, *lih-tze* are used as gifts because the Chinese word (栗子) sounds like another which means "beget children", *lih tze* (立子). The pear, which also has a name similar in sound to the two characters meaning "beget children", also enjoys symbolic significance. Sunflower and pumpkin seeds, gourd and watermelon and the peach also have symbolic significance. While most augur progeny, the peach symbolises immortality. The peach is also a symbol of the vernal sun. Watermelon and other seeds are a popular offering for visitors during Chinese new year celebrations. All these fruits and seeds portend future happiness. The zest of the expressions is a result of the pun on words and names which make these very useful on auspicious occasions when gifts of goodwill are required. Hallmark cards would not have done a better job. The symbols, allusions and puns play a very important part in China's cultural life.

Being round in shape, many of these fruits symbolise family unity. Melons hold out the hope that all members of the family will remain united and like the pomelo are popular during the moon festival. Apples symbolise peace, in part because of their Chinese name (萍果). The first character sounds like the word meaning "peace" (平). The pomelo symbolises luck and prosperity. Limes symbolise good luck and the name of the mandarin orange in Cantonese means "gold". The spiny leaves of the pineapple form a crown; it is yellow in colour which, like the red of the water melon, are both auspicious. Similarly, the yellow of the bananas and their abundance also make them popular offerings. Due to its being available seasonally and then only in limited amounts because it has to be imported, the fresh lychee (荔枝) is not usually a festival offering. Nowadays, canned lychees are more easily available and are a popular Chinese dessert. One of the characters of its name means "branches". For the Chinese, the fruit symbolises the hope that business will branch out and thus bring prosperity.

A wedding ritual, which is now no longer seen except perhaps in mainland China, has been described by Reverend William C. Milne in his 1858 book *Life in China*. The wedding couple would sit in the bridal chamber and throw a plateful of five vari-coloured fruits, berries and confections at their guests and spectators. These berries and fruits symbolise the hope for many children. The custom was apparently instituted some 1900 years ago by an emperor during his wedding. He scattered a tray of fruits and berries at his subjects with the blessing that "as many as these berries as any one can catch, so many children may he have."

Some of the lunar months or twelve moons of the Chinese calendar are named after fruits (Lee Siow Mong in *Spectrum of Chinese Culture*). The literary name of the second moon is *xing* or apricot. That of the third moon is *tao* or peach. The fifth moon is named after the pomegranate, the *liu* while the literary name of the tenth moon is the plum, *mei*. Two other moons are named after food items. The literary name of the sixth moon is lotus or *he* while that of the eighth moon is *qui* or cassia.

On the fifteenth day of the lunar new year celebrations, the elderly would be telling the young women to throw oranges into the water to get good husbands in the future while the young men were supposed to throw apples for good wives. More sceptical people think that the practice gave young women a reason to go out of the house in the past as they were normally not allowed to do so. The rhyming couplet which carries this message is " 抛萍果娶贤妻，抛柑嫁好郎 ".

Sugar cane symbolises shelter for the Hokkiens and pairs of these are often placed behind the door and beside the altar table during the lunar new year celebrations as well as major family events such as weddings. For the latter celebration, sugar cane symbolises a sweet future.

9. The Significance Of Nuts, Beans And Root Vegetables

Though a humble legume, the groundnut is prominent in several Chinese dishes. The nutty flavour (*ma*) is one of the several important flavours taught to a Chinese cook and which he must remember throughout his career. Groundnuts are offered to ancestors because they symbolise continuity, according to Evelyn Lip in her book *Notes on Things Chinese*. Groundnuts are known as *hua sheng* (花生) and *sheng* means "giving birth". As suggested earlier, they are an important item among the offerings used on festive occasions. In their shells and sun-dried, they are a favourite accompaniment to Chinese wine and tea. Groundnuts are sometimes cooked in the gravy of pork broth seasoned with soya sauce and five-spice powder and served as an hors-d'oeuvre. Some are salted or spiced and then dried.

Steamed or boiled groundnuts are also extremely fragrant and are especially popular on cold days. After shelling, the groundnuts can also be roast-fried with some coarse salt in a wok and eaten with plain rice *congee* though most prefer to fry them lightly in oil and then tossed in salt. A variety of different batters are also used to coat the groundnuts as we have pointed out earlier. These can be sweet or just plain crispy and savoury. One variety, which is coated in sugar dyed pink or left white with dashes of red colouring, is called *kim kong tau*. This is used to make the *bee chian* which is offered together with the roast pig on the ninth day of the Chinese lunar new year celebrations. Pork symbolises prosperity and a fat pig is a symbol of wealth (Evelyn Lip in *Notes on Things Chinese*).

Groundnuts are also used in savoury dishes like soups. In those made from spare-ribs or pig's tail, the nuts are added. *Tor tau lin* (花生仁) soup can also be sweet and made from either whole groundnuts or groundnut meal, the latter making a thicker gruel-like soup. This groundnut meal soup is a popular dessert. Groundnut meal is also used for a biscuit which is a popular Chinese new year treat. It is also used in *kong tng*, or peanut candy which are rhombus-shaped pieces of groundnut meal and sugar.

Chopped up or pounded in a stone mortar, the *cheng ku* (石臼), made from groundnuts which have been roast-fried in a wok, is used in the fillings of several types of Chinese cakes. The *ang koo kueh* (红龟粿) and *bao* (饱) have already been discussed. Another is the *moi chi* (芝麻米团) as well as various cakes like *ban chian kueh* (万煎糕). Both of these cakes are still widely sold by hawkers. The *moi chi* is a pastry made from glutinous rice flour and water. This is then rolled in rice flour, cut into small squares and served with chopped groundnuts or rolled into balls with the sweetened, chopped groundnuts as fillings. The *ban chian kueh* is a pancake in which the sweetened groundnut filling is sandwiched in between two layers of pastry. Like pizza, there are two varieties of *ban chian kueh*. One variety is like the pan pizza where the pastry is soft and thick. In the second type, the pastry is thin and crispy.

Apart from biscuits made from ground peanuts, the whole nuts are also used in biscuits. One type of biscuit is made from groundnuts in a batter made from glutinous rice flour and deep-fried. Another type consists of groundnuts in a dough which is also deep-fried but the biscuit is eaten piping hot and fresh out of the wok.

The chopped-up groundnuts are also sprinkled on the sweet dessert made from little round glutinous rice dumplings, the *tang yuan* (汤圆), eaten during the winter solstice celebration *Tung Chih* (冬至) which marks the coming of the lunar new year. The *tang yuan* symbolises union and happiness, being round and sweet (Evelyn Lip in *Notes on Things Chinese*). For the *Tung Chih* festival, twelve larger *tang yuan* are made especially for the religious offerings. These special *tang yuan* symbolise the past twelve months of the year. Chopped groundnuts add substance and fragrance to the dessert. These rice dumplings are cooked in sugar syrup in which *pandan* leaves are sometimes added for extra flavour. More often, slices of ginger are added and this imparts a pleasant tangy flavour to the dessert. Symbolically, the eating of this rice dessert adds a year to the person's age which in the old days was considered a good thing since age was a much venerated asset. Alas, it is not so these days and a number of people have avoided eating these dumplings because of the symbolic significance of the dessert.

The Teochew version of the glutinous rice dumplings called *ar bo leng* are made slightly different. The rice dumplings usually contain sweet stuffing like red bean or mung bean paste, sweet yam or ground peanut. They are also cooked in sugar syrup. Glutinous rice dumplings, *huan-twan* (丸团), were offered in the past during Chinese new year celebrations. The word *huan* (丸) sounds the same as another in the word *huan-hsi* (欢喜) meaning "great joy". Such words signify good omen and augur prosperity and happiness throughout the coming year (Henry Dore in *Researches into Chinese Superstitions*).

Other types of nuts like the gingko nuts and lotus seeds are as versatile as the groundnut although slightly more expensive and therefore considered as luxury foods. Both can be used in a variety of sweet and savoury dishes. They are added to red bean soup as sweet dessert. Lotus seeds boiled in sugar syrup used to be served as a sweet. Savoury soups also have them. A soup which is made from the pig's small intestine and gingko nuts is not only highly palatable but many elderly people believe it is very good for those with weak bladders. Accordingly, many parents have been known to prepare this soup for their children when they are taking their school examinations.

Root Vegetables

These vegetables are humble fare like the groundnut but they make very good eating for the poor beside being versatile and inexpensive. Reverend Justus Doolittle in his 1864 book *The Social Life of the Chinese* reported that among the Chinese, it was considered a hardship and a mark of excessive poverty to eat sweet potatoes except as lunch. Large quantities of potatoes would be grated into coarse strips and dried in the sun, for use as food among the poor in case rice could not be obtained.

The root vegetables are also carved into decorative shapes which are then used as garnishes. Such a use of root vegetables must have been strictly reserved for court and government dishes. In the past, an added advantage was that they could be used to make dumplings which could then be eaten as an alternative to rice in order to weather that season in between rice harvests especially when the rice stock might be running low. The root vegetables were easier and faster to grow and usually did not require very fertile land. Generally regarded as a poor man's fare they were nonetheless used in food offered during festivals and celebrations. Calling a person a *han chu tai* or sweet potato *tai* is as derogatory as calling him a rice bin since both essentially mean that he is an idiot.

One of the most commonly eaten root vegetable is sweet potato. There are several varieties, the yellow and the orange being just some of them. The sweet potato can be eaten plain, simply boiled or roasted in the embers of slow charcoal fires. In China, the farmers used to ensure that their sweet potatoes would be good for eating by sprinkling coal ashes over them. Cut up into big pieces the sweet potatoes make a sweet soup dessert which can be flavoured with ginger and is still extremely popular as a dessert. What is more, it is filling and easy to fix, a dessert which even poor families can provide for their children. Sweet potatoes in sugar threads was a popular dessert in the past.

Sweet potatoes are also often added to rice congee, adding both colour and flavour. Sliced, they can be made into fritters. The Chinese have also found the sweet potato leaf good to eat, either stir-fried on its own or with shrimps and pork. In one spicy dish, the leaves are stir-fried with hot bean paste or *sambal*.

A popular Hokkien savoury dish is the sweet potato dumpling (蕃薯园) which is fashioned from sweet potato and flour and then shaped into a little bow or boomerang, with a peanut in the middle of the bow. The sweet potatoes are boiled, mashed and mixed with flour before being shaped into bows. They are steamed and kept aside until they are ready for use. They are usually fried with thin slivers of pork, spring onions, shrimps and crab meat. The Shanghainese have a similar type of rice dumpling in their *ningko* (年糕) but these are made of rice flour and water. The dumplings are then cut into slices and dried. Before they are cooked, the rice dumpling slices have to be soaked overnight in water to soften and reconstitute them. The rice dumpling is also fried with pork, spring onions, shrimps and crab meat. Eating *ningko* during the Chinese new year festival has significance for the Shanghainese as it symbolises the hope for yearly increase and achievements.

Sweet potato is also used to make the skin wrapping of *bao*. The filling consists of stir-fried root vegetables like shredded radish and carrot mixed with shrimp and pork. The sweet potato *bao* is steamed and offered during Chinese festivals. It is lightly fried before it is eaten.

Just as popular in many families' repertoire of Hokkien dishes are yam dumplings (芋角) which are also specialties conjured up to add to the number of dishes and the spread for the monthly food offerings to the spirits at the back of the home (游魂). The making of the yam dumplings is simple and yet the results look as intricate and decorative as those fashioned out of sweet potatoes. The yam is shredded and then mixed with tapioca and some plain flour with sufficient water to hold the yam together. Then the mix is shaped into ovals the size of an adult's hand. These oval dumplings are then steamed. They are sliced thinly after they have been cooled and are ready for eating. Then they are fried in oil. The amount of oil used is just sufficient to cover the bottom of the wok. They are crispy and as good as potato chips when freshly fried and hot or they can be eaten just like the sweet potato dumplings, stir-fried with shallots, pork, shrimps and crab meat.

Yams also come in several varieties. They symbolise fertility and some dialect groups eat them during the moon-cake festival which falls on the fifteenth day of the eighth lunar month. These yams are believed to be able to strengthen the eyesight and also prevent trans-migration of the soul. The yams are eaten with moon-cakes and water caltrops, *ling-kioh* (菱角). Small varieties of yams are usually just steamed for eating. These yams are eaten with raw sugar. They are also used in broths and braised leg of pork. The large variety of yams can also be used in these. Large yams are used in different versions of yam cakes as described earlier.

Yam is shredded and used for the skin wrapping of *bao* in which are fillings made from other root vegetables like radishes and carrots, stir-fried with shrimps and pork. The *bao* is then steamed and can be kept for serving later. It is usually lightly fried before serving. It is also often part of the monthly religious offerings to the spirits at the back of the home. Ordinary mortals usually eat the fried yam *bao* for breakfast. A Cantonese pastry *woo kok* is made from yam paste which is used for the skin wrapping of a *bao* in which stir-fried chopped pork and prawns are stuffed. The *woo kok* is then deep-fried. The same yam paste has also been fashioned in baskets and deep-fried. These are used to serve stir-fried vegetables in.

Pieces of yam are sometimes added to rice. The yam rice is usually flavoured with soya sauce and eaten with a seafood soup or other types of soup. Like the pieces of steamed yam cake which is added to Chinese noodles, *chee cheong fun*, the yam gives extra fragrance to the rice and also makes it more substantial.

Sliced yam can be steamed for eating with sugar or made into fritters and dipped in sugar or just eaten without any extras. Yam paste is also one of the main ingredients in the popular Teochew dessert *or ni* (芋泥). In this dessert, yam paste is mixed with pumpkin and gingko nuts. Yam can also be used to make yam fries as well and indeed some baskets are fashioned not from yam paste but yam fries. Yam paste is also used in local-style pretzels which is among many of the offerings seen during Chinese new year festivities.

The white radish is just as versatile. It is used for soups together with pork or pork ribs. The shredded vegetable is also the main ingredient of carrot cake (菜头粿) which is popular as a local breakfast dish. The radish symbolises abundance since the *luo* character in the Chinese name (萝) means "abundance". Radishes fried with *bee hoon*, a white rice flour noodle, used to be a favourite dish among the Chinese farmers. The *bee hoon* and radishes are fried with soya sauce as the seasoning. In the old days in China when food was scarce, leaves from the radish were also popular in the Chinese diet. The leaves were salted and then placed in pottery urns and jars and covered. They turned pale yellow and crunchy when ready for eating.

Turnips have been included in the Chinese diet and are good to eat just raw with either sweet and hot bean paste spread all over each slice or just plain chilli sauce. They are indispensable in local varieties of salad like *rojak*. The Chinese varieties of this salad have included ingredients like sliced-up *yu-tiao*. More strictly Chinese is the salad called *jiu he char* (鱿鱼炒). This salad can be eaten on its own as a vegetable dish or in *po piah* (薄饼). The salad is made from shredded turnips and carrots which have been braised with slices of pork, shrimps and dried cuttlefish. This salad is the most important ingredient in *po piah*. Turnips are also used in soups.

Another root vegetable which is popular in soups is the lotus root. Slices of the root are usually added to spare rib soup. Finely sliced pieces of the lotus root have been cooked and sweetened to be eaten as an hors-d'oeuvre. Lotus root balls have also been mentioned in books on Chinese food.

Tapioca makes great cakes which are *peranakan* rather than strictly Chinese. The traditional way of fixing these cakes was to pour the mix of tapioca, *santan* and sugar into tins lined with banana leaves. They are then baked in charcoal stoves over which the hot coals are heaped. Another way of making a tapioca snack is to steam it and then cook it in coconut milk and *gula melaka*. Sliced, the tapioca can be made into fritters. It can also be used to make chips. A starch made from tapioca flour is added to local Chinese dessert such as *bubur cha cha*, a coconut milk-based soup to which are added pieces of yam and sweet potatoes together with sago and *pandan* leaves for flavouring. Tapioca flour is also used in batters for meat dumplings and is often a cheaper substitute for cornflour.

Soya Beans and the Beans Used in Chinese Food

The things which can be done with the versatile *doufu* and their high protein content have been the subject of much discussion. Although a staple ingredient of Chinese diet and available practically in every region, the bean curd and bean curd cakes do not appear to be so highly regarded. This may account for why they are not often seen among ceremonial offerings. Being compared to a a a piece of bean curd is far from complimentary as it means being soft and spineless or a weakling. Despite this, bean curd cakes are highly versatile since you can steam them, braise and fry the many varieties which are available. They can also be stuffed with meat or salads and used as a dish or snack. Generally bland on their own, they can be added to broths and soups for extra bite and substance when feeding a hungry family.

There are fifteen types of bean curd which are of varying consistency. Some types are extremely soft while others are firmer. There are also dry types of bean curd which are popular in soups and stir-fried dishes as well as Chinese-style curries and *rojak*, the local salad. The soft and watery types of bean curd are often steamed or used in soups. Firmer types are used in braised dishes, fried or stuffed and then fried.

The not so bland Hakka-style *tau keow* (豆干) is made from fermented beans which give the two varieties commonly sold, their distinctive flavour. Rectangular in shape, one type is coloured an uncompromising black and the other golden brown.

Bean curd sheets *tau kee* or *foo pei* (豆支) are an ingredient of sweet desserts and broths or soups. They are also much used as wrappings in Chinese-style turnovers and patties. Deep-fried, they are fragrant and crispy. They are also used in a bean and barley drink where the bean curd sheets are cooked with barley and gingko nuts. Chinese families prepare it for a cooling drink. There are a few kinds of *foo pei*. The long yellow sheets are most commonly used, especially in preparing the Hokkien prawn roll in which chopped prawns are rolled in a bean curd sheet and then deep-fried. Those brown squares of bean curd sheets, which are quite uncommon, are usually cut into strips and fried as a snack or added to salads and other stir-fried vegetable dishes.

Fermented beans like the *tau kiam* or *tau loo* (豆乳) are favourites with the elderly when they take rice *congee*. A more familiar name for this food would be beancurd cheese (*furu*). It is prepared from fermented beans which is made into a paste. The *tau kiam* is also good added to braised dishes of pork, chicken or fish. Another type of salted fermented soya bean paste (豆浆) is also used with braised fish dishes to mask the fishiness and add flavour. Fermented black soya beans are also used for this purpose. Red soya beans are used to make a sweet bean paste. Broad beans are used in savoury bean pastes. These bean pastes are used for marinades and seasoning in Chinese dishes.

Unlike the spices used in several Chinese dishes which are not native to China, the soya beans originate from China. They have been part of Chinese cooking for the last 4,000 years or so.

The Chinese have devised several ingenious ways of masking the fishiness of seafood, apart from the use of bean paste. Preserved sour plums are commonly used together with chillies to produce a sweet-sour and hot flavour. The use of these plums is almost as popular as the use of plum sauce for Beijing roast duck. Chinese parsley and ginger are also lavishly sprinkled over the seafood. Equally well-known would be the sweet and sour sauce used for seafood, which is made from blending vinegar, sugar and soya sauce.

Tamarind is not only used to clean new woks before use but cleverly adopted by the overseas Chinese to spice seafood like fish. *Kiam cai* (咸菜), salted Chinese cabbage, is also a common ingredient in fish and duck dishes. If not applied to food, it generally means things which have been mauled over (like clothes on sale in large departmental stores, flung hither and thither). Salted fish is also similarly applied in non-food contexts to unwashed shoes. The Hokkiens are even more explicit, leaving little to the imagination in their term *chao kiam hu* (臭咸鱼) meaning smelly salted fish. A variety of black beans is often used in soup made from pig's tail and is apparently excellent for "wind", a condition commonly associated with rheumatism.

Sweet and hot (as in pepper hot) bean paste, all the red and black varieties, are also condiments much used for flavouring and seasoning. Both soya and broad beans are ingredients used in the paste. The ketchup must have started out this way as well. These different varieties of bean paste are also used as marinades for chicken and other meats. Red bean paste especially, gives the much desired red colouring to marinaded roasted chicken.

BIBLIOGRAPHY

Bredon, J. and I. Mitrophanow, *The Moon Year — A Record of Chinese Customs and Festivals*, Shanghai: Kelly and Walsh Ltd, 1927.

China, The Beautiful Cookbook, Hong Kong: International Publishing Corporation, 1986.

Clayre, A., *Heart of the Dragon*, London: Dragonbook ApS, 1984.

Doolittle, J., *Social Life of the Chinese: With some Account of their Religious, Governmental, Educational and Business Customs and Opinions*, Vol 1, New York: Harper and Brothers (Original Edition), 1865.

Dore, H., *Researches into Chinese Superstitions*, Vols I-III and IV-V, Taipei: Ch'eng-Wen Publishing Co., 1966. (Translated from French with notes, historical and explanatory by M. Kennelly.)

Dore, H., *Researches into Chinese Superstitions*, Vols VI-VIII, Taipei: Ch'eng-Wen Publishing Co., 1967. (Translated from French with notes, historical and explanatory by M. Kennelly.)

Dore, H., *Researches into Chinese Superstitions*, Vols IX-X, Taipei: Ch'eng-Wen Publishing Co., 1967. (Translated by D.J. Finn.)

Douglas, R.K., *Society in China*, London: A.D. Innes & Co., 1894.

Greenberg, S. and Ortiz, E.L., *Book of Spices*, Singapore: Times Books International, 1984 (Southeast Asian edition).

Kiang Kang-Hu, *Chinese Civilisation: An Introduction to Sinology*, Shanghai, China: Chung Hwa Book Co., 1935.

Langdon, W.B., *Ten Thousand Things Related to China and the Chinese: An Epitome of the Genius, Government, History, Literature, Agriculture, Arts, Trade, Manners, Customs and Social Life of the People of the Celestial Empire*, London: Chinese Collection, Hyde Park Corner, 1843.

Lee Siow Mong, *Spectrum of Chinese Culture*, Petaling Jaya, Malaysia: Pelanduk Publications (M) Sdn Bhd, 1986.

Lip, E., *Notes on Things Chinese*, Singapore: Graham Brash, 1988.

Lu Shu (ed.), *Famous Chinese Recipes*, Hong Kong: Food Paradise Publishing, 1984.

MacGowan, J., *Men and Manners of Modern China*, London: T. Fisher Unwin, 1912.

Milne, W.C., *Life in China*, London: G. Routledge & Co., 1858.

Reitlinger, G., *South of the Clouds — A Winter Ride Through Yunnan*, London: Faber and Faber Ltd, (undated).

Sues, I.R., *Sharks' Fins and Millet*, Garden City, New York: Garden City Publishing Co., 1944.

UNESCO, *China: Past and Present, Cultures: Dialogue between Peoples of the World*, 34/35, 1984.

Wilhelm, R., *The Soul of China*, London: Jonathan Cape, (undated). (Text translated by John Holroyd Reece.)